Teaching languages online

MM Textbooks

MM Textbooks bring the subjects covered in our successful range of academic monographs to a student audience. The books in this series explore education and all aspects of language learning and use, as well as other topics of interest to students of these subjects. Written by experts in the field, the books are supervised by a team of world-leading scholars and evaluated by instructors before publication. Each text is student-focused, with suggestions for further reading and study questions leading to a deeper understanding of the subject.

Full details of all the books in this series and of all our other publications can be found on http://www.multilingual-matters.com, or by writing to Multilingual Matters, St Nicholas House, 31-34 High Street, Bristol BS1 2AW, UK.

MM Textbooks

Teaching languages online

Carla Meskill and Natasha Anthony

MULTILINGUAL MATTERS
Bristol • Buffalo • Toronto

Library of Congress Cataloging in Publication Data
A catalog record for this book is available from the Library of Congress.

Meskill, Carla.
Teaching Languages Online/Carla Meskill and Natasha Anthony.
MM Textbooks: 6
Includes bibliographical references and index.
1. Language and languages--Study and teaching--Technological innovations. 2. Language and languages--Computer-assisted instruction. 3. Intercultural communication--Study and teaching--Data processing. 4. Web-based instruction. 5. Educational technology. I. Anthony, Natasha. II. Title.
P53.28.M48 2010
418.0078'5–dc22 2010005057

British Library Cataloguing in Publication Data
A catalogue entry for this book is available from the British Library.

ISBN-13: 978-1-84769-272-6 (hbk)
ISBN-13: 978-1-84769-271-9 (pbk)

Multilingual Matters
UK: St Nicholas House, 31-34 High Street, Bristol BS1 2AW, UK.
USA: UTP, 2250 Military Road, Tonawanda, NY 14150, USA.
Canada: UTP, 5201 Dufferin Street, North York, Ontario M3H 5T8, Canada.

The policy of Multilingual Matters/Channel View Publications is to use papers that are natural, renewable and recyclable products, made from wood grown in sustainable forests. In the manufacturing process of our books, and to further support our policy, preference is given to printers that have FSC and PEFC Chain of Custody certification. The FSC and/or PEFC logos will appear on those books where full certification has been granted to the printer concerned.

Typeset by Saxon Graphics Ltd, Derby
Printed and bound in Great Britain by the MPG Books Group

Contents

1

Teaching languages well online: the essentials

- This initial chapter discusses the fundamental concepts involved in online language teaching and introduces the approach and format for the proceeding chapters.

- With the focus in this and subsequent chapters being on active teaching in online venues, foundations of task design and their orchestration via instructional conversations are established.

- The chapter supplies definitions for the four online language learning environments and their affordances.

- Fundamentals of designing task toolkits for online language teaching are outlined and illustrated.

Teaching languages well online: the essentials

There is no question that teaching and learning languages online is growing in popularity. The reasons for this growth are many. Chief among them is the matter of convenience. Rather than traveling distances short and long to participate in face-to-face (f2f) courses, people wishing to study a new language have only to turn to their computer screens any hour of the day or night and access instruction. The forms that this instruction takes are many and varied; some depending on instructors, some depending on stand-alone instructional materials, and many both. Moreover, many language educators who teach in the traditional f2f classroom are making good use of online tools and materials as complements to their courses, places where students can practice and study outside of class time. In short, the amount of instructional activity taking place in cyberspace is enormous and, as we hope you will find in this text, enormously exciting.

Those who are skeptical about online learning tend to point to the loss of the fast-paced, stimulating interaction that takes place in live language classrooms. It is true that the timing and with it the dynamics of interactions is radically different, however, as we explore throughout this text, there are numerous affordances that can, when exploited by excellent instruction, mitigate the absence of live interaction. Indeed, since we first began teaching online several years ago, students report that where they once enjoyed the pacing and adrenaline of live classes, they find the timing element in online forums more to their liking. This is especially true for learners who are less outgoing in live contexts; the luxury of time and quasi-anonymity work in their favor. Language learners who might otherwise not react well under the pressure of real-time comprehension and production particularly enjoy online language learning.

What this book is about

This text lays out methods and their rationale for optimal uses of online environments for effective language teaching. It primarily addresses professional language educators, those new to the field, those with experience in traditional classrooms, and those who teach partly or fully online. Our three foundational premises are as follows:

- Language learning is made up of primarily social/instructional processes.

- Online environments can be used well socially and instructionally.

- Teaching well in online environments requires skilled instruction.

We therefore focus on the kinds of teacher instructional moves in conversation with students, what we call, along with Tharp and Gallimore (1991), 'instructional conversations' that in our work are proving highly effective for teaching language in online environments. Before expanding further on these three foundational premises for our approach to online language teaching, we will address some essential practical matters that concern the mechanics and logistics of online teaching: time, management, learning goals and assessment.

Time

Online teaching and learning can take place as it does in a f2f classroom *synchronously*, that is in real time, or *asynchronously*, whenever its participants choose to interact. Both of these teaching modes require conceptualizations of time that are quite different from traditional meet-four-times-a-week planning and participation structures. In the short term, the design and planning of online elements is time consuming. In the long term, however, the fact of having all materials and structures in a single place is a time saver. In regard to the actual teaching/contact time with students, online teaching is often viewed as requiring more time than face-to-face as instead of having contact with students three to four times per week, one is having contact every day. And, as mentioned earlier, students who would otherwise shy away from actively participating in f2f contexts are more than likely contributing more and more often for reasons we will discuss shortly. This in turn compels instructors to be more actively and continuously responsive throughout the term. While instructors are quick to point out these time investments, they are also quick to qualify these by citing other areas where enormous amounts of time are saved. We mentioned having all one's course materials in one place. In addition, there is the matter of convenience. Many online instructors log onto their courses when it suits their schedules; not at 11:00 a.m. every Tuesday, Wednesday and Thursday but rather some days evenings, some mornings as their schedules permit. Traveling to and from a physical classroom, parking, meals away from home, even clothing and childcare can all be factored in to counterbalance the time investment in online education. Most instructors who calculate and consider the shifts in how their time is spent testify to the increase in the quality time they can spend teaching well in exchange for time spent on activity extraneous to actual instruction.

Students also enjoy the time savings of doing online learning. For many contemporary students, the time and logistics of traveling to a physical classroom according to a set schedule can be challenging. Students who work and who have families can study anytime and anywhere that suits their busy schedules. There are the larger life time issues and then there is the matter of instructional time itself.

Instructional time

In addition to available time (above), this text is particularly interested in instructional time; that is, the time that both instructors and learners have to carefully consider the form and content of their online postings in online venues. For learners, it is within this thinking, comprehending and composing time that active language learning is taking place. For instructors, it is within this thinking, comprehending and composing time that optimal instructional conversation moves can be devised given the current status of the class discussion. Both students and their teachers can, moreover, use this time to access any and all information they need to comprehend, compose and instruct. For students, the most obvious example might be taking advantage of online resources such as dictionaries, thesauruses and even native speaker friends in composing their posts. For instructors, they can access and in turn make use of background cultural information and artifacts, visuals, animated grammar explications and the like to amplify their instructional conversation moves.

Task design

Like in the traditional f2f language classroom, a major part of instructional routines involves tasks in which learners engage with the aim of their practicing and thus learning target language forms and functions. A language learning task can be thought of as a structured activity that has clear instructional objectives, content and context that is culturally authentic and appropriate, and specified procedures for its undertaking. Tasks are, then, activities in which learners engage for the purpose of mastering aspects of the target language under study. They range in complexity from brief language workouts (e.g. listen and repeat, listen or read and perform a grammatical transformation) to more complex activities such as role play simulations, group decision-making or sustained interactions with native speakers for problem solving. The essential element that defines language learning tasks is the purpose, objective or outcome of the task, an element that we will stress throughout this text. It is through a consistent focus on task objectives that teachers make productive use of instructional conversation moves to guide and enhance the learning.

```
Sample Language Learning Task Template
Topic:
Duration:
Skills focus:
Overall instructional aims:
Task structure:
        Task toolkit
        Roles for learners
        Setting the scene
        Action expectations
        Action monitoring → instructional conversation (feedback)
Expected outcomes
```

Figure 1 Sample language learning task template

The *task toolkit* is a convention that we use throughout this text. It is the set of language elements that make up the focus of a given language task. One advantage of online instruction in this regard is that these toolkits can be collected and managed in a course task repository and reused as needed. The information in the task toolkit should be as simple and direct as possible as it is to these language elements that instructors and students refer as they undertake and evaluate the processes and outcomes of the given task. Our convention is to place this boxed text in the upper right-hand corner of all screens as a consistent anchoring and referencing tool (Figure 2).

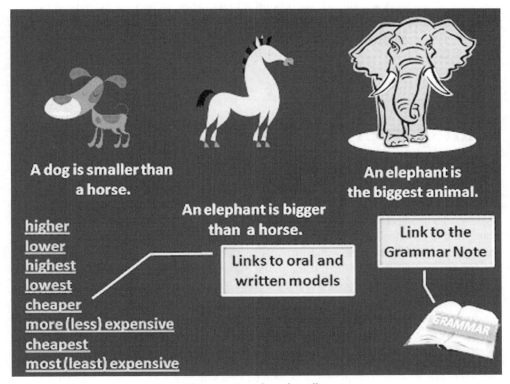

Figure 2 Sample task toolkit

Roles for learners can be specified much as they are in the live classroom. In online environments, however, one can also provide links to background language and cultural information concerning the roles that learners are assigned. If, for example, a student is assigned the role of a bank manager in a bank robbery role play, links to target culture sites and information (video clips are particularly useful in understanding target culture social roles) can be included in the description of the particular assigned role. In this way also learners can have background about one another's roles so as to better attune their communication patterns with one another.

Similarly, in *setting the scene* for a language learning task, students and instructors have at their fingertips massive amounts of background information in multimodal forms. Taking the bank robbery role play task as an example, learners can see and explore banks and banking routines in the target culture as part of preparing to undertake the task.

Action expectations and *action monitoring* constitute the heart of powerful instructional conversations. As you will see throughout the text, this aspect of language learning tasks is where we believe the real teaching and learning occur. Learners are expected to comprehend and produce specified language correctly (action expectations) and instructors monitor accordingly. In monitoring these task-guided conversations, instructors seek out teachable moments – moments where learners need a push, a reminder, reference to the task goals and/or task toolkit, or probes of their understanding of target culture and context. These teachable moments represent rich opportunities in online environments in terms of time and available resources, as we discussed above. We will discuss the goals and anatomy of instructional conversations more thoroughly at the end of this chapter and, subsequently, illustrate these throughout the remaining chapters.

Management

Managing ten to thirty students three or four times per week in traditional classroom settings is onerous. How does one manage the learning in online environments? As mentioned earlier, the sheer fact of having all of one's materials, all student work, all archives of what has taken place in one online location is a great time saver in the long term. Being able to revisit what has already occurred in class over time can be a powerful management tool in assisting with future instructional planning as well. Managing all of this information can be facilitated through the use of a Course Management System (CMS) whereby special tools are provided to track learners, their assignments, their participation structures, their contributions. Thus, the kinds of continually and automatically updated information about online learning activity can greatly ease the overall management of coursework that takes place online.

An element of management that can in large part determine the level of success for an online course or online component of a course is the setting of norms and expectations. Because learners are structuring their own time in these online venues, the amount and quality of their participation for optimal learning, and optimal grades, need to be clearly specified and pointed to throughout the term. Actual models and exemplars of optimal participation structures can be provided so that learners are 100% clear on the mode, purpose and level of quality expected. Reminders of these expectations can be visually present and pointed to throughout the term.

In addition to management, one of the most critical features of online instruction as reported in research studies is the online behaviors of the instructor. When students log on to their course site, they immediately seek out information on the instructor's recent participation. Likewise, anecdotal and formal research accounts point out that students attend most to the posts of instructors and less to the posts of other students. In short, being present and active in the online venue is a critical factor for successful instruction. This means logging on and actively instructing on a consistent, continual basis. Many an online student has reported feeling 'abandoned' when instructors take a day off. Thus, part of the online instructional equation is to 'be present' even if it means announcing that you will be offline for the weekend.

Content/Sequencing

In structuring online content and activities, instructors can use a variety of approaches, just like in traditional f2f classes. If the course is structured around the content and sequence of a textbook, support materials and activities can be likewise sequenced. One of the most common uses of an online portion of a language course is to use online discussion spaces as a place for learners to engage in complementary tasks and activities that align with textbook units. In this way online portions are used to support and amplify the content under study. A fully online course can be structured in a like manner. In many cases language textbook publishers provide online supplementary and support activities that can be incorporated and used to structure the online portion of a language course.

The breadth of any language course is, of course, dependent on its length of study and goals. The depth, however, when undertaken all or in part on the internet, is potentially limitless. Reference, background and expansion materials abound. Making good, sound use of these limitless content possibilities starts with examining the purposes and goals of the tasks and activities that make up the course. Websites from the target language and culture can be effectively repurposed and mined for use by learners as the basis of communicative language learning tasks. Examples of ways to make use of these resources appear throughout the following chapters.

Assessment

Micro-level

Because language learning is a dynamic and multifaceted enterprise, one that is influenced by any number of individual and contextual factors, in this text we advocate the centrality of ongoing formative assessment of student learning. In this view, the two – instruction and assessment – are viewed as interdependent. As an instructor is evaluating learner comprehension and performance, it is on this evaluation that she bases the construction of her subsequent instructional moves, her instruction in essence. This marriage of instruction/assessment happens in instructional conversations where opportunities for authentic interaction in the target language are orchestrated and overseen by an instructor with specific plans and goals. Her responses to learners as they undertake her activities are responsive to her assessment of learner performance and, thereby, learner readiness in a given teachable moment. This is instruction that pushes a learner along his or her developmental trajectory towards mastery of the focal target language (Meskill, 2009).

Task → learner post → instructor assessment → instructional conversation move → learner post

Macro-level

Online venues are excellent ones for tracking learner progress. Whether you use a free and open communication forum or a sophisticated CMS, you will have digital records of student performance. These can be in the form of graded exercises, essays and other kinds of individual assignments. Assessments can also be made of the threaded discourse contributions learners have made while undertaking tasks and while responding to instructor prompts and guidance. These kinds of running records of learner growth and development in the new language take assessment to a new and quite powerful level as they supply archived information upon which to base subsequent instruction, something the most expert teacher would have difficulty tracking in f2f venues. These digital records, moreover, can serve as a guide for learners themselves to gain a sense of their strengths, weaknesses and overall progress. Collecting exemplary moments in class discussions and learning tasks and assembling these in a student-generated electronic portfolio is an excellent instructional strategy both in terms of student learning and in conserving instructor time for actual teaching.

The four environments

When setting out to learn on the internet, we can simply interact with the materials and resources available via searching and referencing information. We can also make use of widely available digital learning objects (DLOs). These are materials that are explicitly instructional and, in most cases, interactive: games, tutorials, fill in the blank, videos, teaching animations, drills, simulations and the like. What marks these as DLOs is their *instructional* purpose. Numerous online DLO repositories curate collections of these objects for more streamlined access by educators (http://merlot.org, for example). These kinds of learning objects can be assigned to learners for independent work. They can also be incorporated into online coursework whereby students are assigned collaborative tasks that make use of these learning objects thereby serving as springboards or catalysts for instructional interactions between and among learners and instructors.

In addition to online materials in the form of digital learning objects, there are four venues for teaching and learning online, each with its distinct characteristics and affordances (Figure 3): written asynchronous, written synchronous, oral asynchronous and oral synchronous.

Written asynchronous environments are likely the most familiar to anyone who uses telecommunications. Email is the quintessential written asynchronous venue whereby messages are composed and comprehended outside of real time, much as a letter or postcard sent via land mail. In written asynchronous learning environments, learners read and respond to posts made by their instructor and their fellow students when it is convenient to do so. For online instruction, this mode or venue is by far the most popular. This is in great part due to the fact that instruction can be accessed and engaged at any time from any location. It is for this reason, written asynchronous is the most widely used mode of online instructional delivery by educational institutions around the world. Indeed, the majority of Learning Management Systems (LMS) – software whereby one can build and orchestrate instruction – are designed for the written asynchronous mode of instruction.

Written synchronous environments can be readily compared to Instant Messaging (IM) or texting. Interlocutors compose and comprehend messages in real time. The resulting posts are naturally shorter, less thoughtfully composed and more conversation-like in their form and content. As we will see, written synchronous communication often accompanies oral synchronous communication whereby side conversations take place via text while the main focus of a learning session is oral and synchronous. Written synchronous messaging can also take place in learning environments that are otherwise written asynchronous. Most LMSs have a chat-like feature that can be used by prior arrangement for real-time interactions.

Affordances of asynchronous online teaching and learning environments

– convenience
– connectivity
– membership (playing field is leveled)
– authentic audiences
– tailored audiences
– strategies to compensate for lack of non-verbal info
– richness of information (links, multimedia)
– time to focus and review
– time to compose, resources to compose
– time and opportunity to reflect
– opportunity to witness and track learning
– opportunity to demonstrate learning

Affordances of synchronous online teaching and learning environments

– convenience
– connectivity
– membership (playing field is leveled)
– authentic audiences
– tailored audiences
– richness of information (links, multimedia)
– opportunity to witness and track learning in real time
– opportunity to demonstrate learning in real time

Figure 3 Affordances of online teaching and learning environments

Oral asynchronous environments are popular for informal learning on the web. Similar to blogs, posters can record and post their thoughts, questions and responses to others via audio. Similarly, recorded audio posts can be inserted into just about any online environment, page or document for instructional purposes. Audio responses to written compositions, for example, can be inserted as a means of feedback. Recorded audio commentary can also accompany student products such as poster sessions, gallery tours of portfolio work or other multimodal creations. Likewise, instructors can insert their recordings of mini-lectures within their written asynchronous materials. Further, as we will see, oral synchronous becomes particularly attractive for teaching aural/oral skills in another language.

Finally, and perhaps the most robust of online instructional environments, **oral synchronous environments** are marked by combining multiple modalities in real time. This is the most demanding environment for instructors and students as attention is simultaneously drawn to real-time speech, real-time visual information and synchronous written messages. Learners and instructor log on at the same time to interact in ways similar to the live classroom. Information is visually represented and manipulated by the instructor while she speaks. Responses from learners are elicited and responded to. Pair and groupwork are assigned, orchestrated and evaluated. As with the other three online environments, sessions can be recorded and archived for later reference by both learners and instructors.

Blended learning

Blended learning, whereby live in-class time is supplemented or supplanted by either synchronous or asynchronous online work, is also growing in popularity. There are several scheduling/design schemes one can use for blended instruction:

- *front-loaded* whereby online work leads up to the live sessions in terms of learner preparation;

- *book-ended* whereby live class meetings are bracketed at the beginning and end by online sessions;

- *intermixed* whereby live class meetings are interspersed or replaced with online sessions.

When well planned and well strategized, there are numerous advantages to blended forms of course design. Conversations that require reading, reflection and careful composing can be allocated to asynchronous online sessions; those that thrive on more rapid-fire give and take can be allocated to live meetings. Also, use of an online course space to complement live sessions means that less productive work (managerial, documents' review, etc.) can happen online thus allowing more time for the kinds of live conversations that make sense to particular instructional aims.

Learning community

A focus on active, authentic language use as a means to acquired literacy and fluency can best be undertaken in environments conducive to productive communication. Instructional environments where learners are at ease with their developing new language and new language identities are a central concern in language education. A major affordance of all online learning venues is the fact that learners can exercise their new language in environments where they are safe, valued and, perhaps most importantly, members of a learning community. That sense of membership helps in authentic practice with target language use. Language is, after all, used in and by communities. In language education contexts, these communities are the venues where members are invested in the common goal of acquiring and mastering a new language through its productive use. These are communities whereby instructors play the practical role of curricula and activities determiners, designers of instructional tasks through which curricular goals are met, and orchestrators and guides of moment-by-moment language learning routines or instructional conversations.

Building rapport and a sense of community while not being in the physical company of others can at first appear to be enormously challenging. But, if one considers the quick and undirected proliferation of informal online communities – communities that form around myriad common goals, interests and opinions – digital natives (see below, pp. 13–14) may be more comfortable and adept at online community membership than face-to-face. Indeed, as communicators we seem to do just fine forming and maintaining social relationships synchronously and asynchronously online. Moreover, we increasingly seem to enjoy doing so as a major form of social activity. These pleasures, along with the multimodal literacy skills now commonplace for both digital natives and immigrants, are important to consider, and ways to capitalize on them are integrated throughout this text.

All of these instructional modes or environments boast special features and affordances that are particularly attractive to language education. Taking best advantage of the features and affordances of each is the focus of this text. Before addressing these, we situate our discussion in our broader view of how we see language as best taught and learned.

A sociocultural view of language teaching and learning

The historical shifts away from teaching language in the abstract to teaching language *in use* have been significant. Where language was once treated as a subject area, the substance of which was to be *talked about*, contemporary views see the goal of language instruction to be active, productive *use* of the new language. With these shifts have come reconceptualizations of just what it means to acquire and know a language well, along with reconsideration of what teaching and learning processes best effect this.

Chomsky's 1965 critical distinction between language performance and language competence – a distinction that explains our ability to judge grammaticality (competence) while at the same time making mistakes in our speaking and writing (performance) –

forms the basis of Dell Hymes's later characterization of the complexities of language use via his definition of *communicative competence*. In order to demonstrate communicative competence, Hymes argued, a speaker must say the right thing, in the right way with the right effect given a specific communicative situation and all of its contextual complexities (Goodwin & Duranti, 1992; Hymes, 1971, 1972). This notion of competence represented a sea change in our conceptions about what it meant to *know* or *speak* another language well. In the decades leading up to Hymes's insight, learning another language often meant learning to read, perhaps translate, and rarely involved communicative proficiency. Professional language educators, researchers in applied linguistics and publishers actively responded to Hymes's insight by developing materials, methods and research methodologies that aligned with this view of language competence. Shortly thereafter Sandra Savignon coined this new, overall approach 'communicative language teaching' (CLT), a moniker which is used to this day to describe language educators' efforts to nurture full communicative competence in their second and foreign language learners (Savignon, 1983, 1991).

Growing interest in Vygotsky's views of learning has begun to influence language education as well (e.g. Lantolf & Pavlenko, 1995). A sociocultural view sees learning as dynamic, ongoing and developing throughout the life span with critical influences coming from the surrounding social order writ both large and local. The act of teaching from this perspective is primarily that of mediation whereby a learner is guided to appropriation and internalization of meaning within the social environment, an environment that has been shaped and continues to shape ways of being and communicating. Many argue that this sociocultural view is entirely compatible with earlier communicative views of language education (e.g. Block, 2003; Foster & Ohta, 2005; Lantolf, 2000; van Lier, 2000). While varying perspectives and theories related to sociocultural views of learning abound, we limit use and discussion to those that have been laid out in the recent literature as pertaining directly to second and foreign language education generally, and how this view frames our concepts of learning and teaching in online environments particularly.

Two aspects of the sociocultural view of learning align particularly well with what applied linguists generally agree about the process of attaining communicative competence in a new language. First, a sociocognitive view sees learning as dialogic with authentic language in use as the primary mediating tool for learning. So that regardless of the content or task, it is the language used by instructors, peers and, finally, the learner herself that directly steers or *mediates* the learning. Thus, directly comprehending and responding appropriately to language – conversation – is central to all developmental processes. Second, when it comes to learning a new language, by experiencing mediation via the target language, learners also experience the opportunity to internalize the language they experience that can, in turn, be used passively and/or productively by them in novel contexts (Swain, 2000). From an instructional stance, these mediation and internalization (what Vygotsky termed *intermentation*) processes that lead to development of the new language are orchestrated by talented instructors who simultaneously assess where a learner's development lies on the target language trajectory and tailors instructional strategies in such a way as to move the learner along their individual developmental pathway (Lantolf & Poehner, 2008; Meskill, 2009).

Key to viewing learning as a dynamic, developmental process is the notion of guided participation, the kinds of participatory structures that we tend to value in contemporary language education contexts. The design of effective participatory structures guides learners to accomplish tasks through the means of language with the assistance of instructors and peers. Providing this kind of support and assistance is what Tharp and Gallimore have called the *instructional conversation,* an aspect of teaching well online that we hold as central throughout this text.

Why online?

> All learning is socially mediated.
>
> Lev Vygotsky, 1978

Why are more and more people across the globe seeking out instruction online? One part of the answer to this question is quite obvious: it is terribly convenient to type in a search word and have the information one needs in less than a second. And, nowadays, one need only visit a DLO repository to find not just information on a particular topic, but instruction in and about that topic. In short, access to information and instruction is quick, convenient and for the most part sufficient for much of the daily learning we need to do, or is it? In this information/instruction retrieval scenario, what is patently missing is the human teacher, the interlocutor who designs and guides learning processes, the person who engages the learner in *instructional conversations.* In the next sections we will discuss the social/interactional dimension with others as a key attribute to learning online generally and learning language online in particular. First, a word about contemporary learners or 'digital natives'.

Digital natives

Today's language learners come to the task of language learning equipped with any number of highly developed digital literacy skills (Meskill, 2007). These skills develop via interaction with computers and with others using computers. While they are generally considered recreational interactions, the concomitant digital prowess young people develop carries implications for their undertaking the study of foreign and second languages. Take the following skills for example:

Multitasking: making and mentally tracking progress toward more than one goal at a time.

Bookmarking: mentally marking one's progress on one task while shifting to and engaging in one or more others.

Updating: continually making changes to one's tracking and bookmarking.

Self-modulating: tracking the process and progress with what has been defined as one's goal structures.

Conjecturing: making informed guesses as to the likely results of one's actions.

Exploring: taking risks, tolerating ambiguity to discover new territory.

Reading discourse contexts: adapting one's language behaviors to align with a given communication context.

Navigating: holding draft navigational maps in memory while revising routes.

Learning from missteps: gaining understanding from unintended outcomes of one's actions.

Representing: representing one's self in a way that contributes towards meeting one's goals, achieving membership.

Reading others' representations: making judgments about the identity and agendas of what and whom is represented.

Judging: evaluating information, its sources, its veracity.

Filing: deciding the importance of particular information for the moment or for later on.

Backchanneling: providing linguistic or visual cues to others to indicate that you are attending to what they say.

There are likely several additional evolving digital literacy competencies that can be added to this brief list. The importance of these digital native competencies is that they cry out to be exploited in language education! If students undertake some or all of these simultaneously as a matter of course for recreational purposes, then they can be expected to undertake some or all in their pursuit of foreign or second language competence. If they are able to move fluidly from one online context to another, they can be guided to do so in the target language/culture. If they are employing sophisticated skills to manipulate what is on the screen, they can do likewise in practicing and mastering the language(s) they study. Digital natives are well versed in online socializing and collaborating, a main attraction for recreational technologies uses. As we will see throughout this text, instructional tasks that capitalize on the attractiveness of social interactions can enrich and enliven language education.

Appealing to digital natives is not the only reason that online learning makes sense. In conjunction with Vygotsky's crucial observation, that all learning is socially mediated, we can address the question *Why online?* A decade or less ago, a language educator may have viewed the internet as a non-social forum, an unfriendly venue for undertaking language instruction, something that is an otherwise highly social enterprise. With the boom in social networking, however, along with sophisticated CMSs for online instruction, the key notion of learning as social is solidly supportable.

With the advent of online instruction and the myriad instructional possibilities it represents, there arises a central question: What exactly is it that instructors who are accustomed to live, f2f interaction with learners are to *do* in these environments? Should one continue to use the instructional strategies that have served them well in the live classroom, or are there special affordances of the medium that can be exploited and thereby require a shift in instructional thinking and method? If we accept as a given that computers are inherently social machines, most pleasurably used for communication and conversation with others, and that learning is best mediated by instructional conversations, then online can be viewed as an optimal venue for language instruction. Indeed, spectacular results from thoughtful integration of online components into teaching and learning abound. Whether it is an elementary science class where students develop and use the language of scientists to work through and solve problems (Zhang *et al.*, 2007) or foreign language instructional contexts where learners develop and use language to solve authentic problems with native speakers of the language they study (Meskill & Anthony, 2007), student-centered, idea-centered instructional conversations online are proving to be invaluable in effectively apprenticing learners into the discourse practices of the target discipline. By actively engaging in contributive conversations with instructors and others, students experience models and appropriate ways of understanding and using the language of specific, authentic domains. For instructors, this means direct, recordable evidence of student learning that is both quantifiable (e.g. how many times did they employ a concept or linguistic form correctly?) and qualifiable (e.g. how richly embedded are the student's observations in the class readings and discussions?). In this way online instructional conversations provide instructors the on-the-fly formative assessment information that steers subsequent instructional moves and activities. Indeed, teachers have the very information they need regarding both individual learners and the group as a whole that generates the next logical step in their instructional sequencing. Armed with this formative input, instructors know just how to push learners towards specific goals and standards.

In short, where educators have long complained that more process-oriented, student-centered learning activities are messy with the goals and objectives often getting lost amidst the natural chaos of developmental human activity, when undertaken in online environments there is not only a record of the instructional conversations, but also a record of individual and group *progress* towards meeting the instructional goals. Such records can be continually consulted with the luxury of time for review and reflection, time that can be productively used to calculate and compose appropriately targeted instructional conversations.

Traditional forms of f2f classroom discourse

Studies of live classroom discourse reveal that the vast majority of teacher utterances are managerial in nature. This not terribly surprising in teacher-centered classrooms where the onus for most activity is on the person standing at the front of the room! In such a context, teachers spend a good deal of time establishing and maintaining control, directing learners' attention, checking for understanding, correcting, keeping to the topic and moving things along ('Now we are going to...').

That teacher talk is dedicated mostly to management is due to the nature of the classroom itself: a large group of diverse individuals in a single venue whose expectations and the expectations of the larger institution in which the groups reside are that learning will take place in a fairly orderly, undisrupted manner. This is a prodigious task for any individual to orchestrate for extended periods of time. The obvious strategy is to use one's speech to manage and maintain order. How that speech gets used varies according to the goals and dynamics of any given moment. However, there is a particular pattern of teacher talk that seems to predominate in a good deal of live classroom learning. That pattern or routine is known as the Initiation–Response–Evaluation (IRE) sequence, a sequence patently familiar to anyone who has ever sat in a classroom. Decades of research on classroom discourse shows that besides management, this form of talk takes up the majority of class discourse.

Here is a familiar IRE sequence:

Initiation: What is the capital of Afghanistan?

Response: Kabul.

Evaluation: Very good.

Since the IRE label was established by classroom discourse researchers Sinclair and Coulthard in 1975, these routines have been variously called known-answer question routines, inauthentic exchanges and monologic conversations (versus dialogic whereby the information requested and shared is new, not already known). Sinclair and Coulthard later dubbed the third move in such exchanges *feedback*, a term subsequently changed to *follow-up*. They proposed three categories of action that can occur in this slot: *accept/reject*, *evaluate*, and *comment*, with the latter category expanded to include the more specific sub-categories *exemplify*, *expand* and *justify*. Teachers can equally ask a further question to the speaker or any other student in order to obtain a more adequate answer.

Beyond their role in directly evaluating learning, IRE sequences can serve a number of additional purposes as well. For example:

- Buying time.
- Directing a topic.
- Gaining attention.
- Punishing.
- Rewarding.
- Moving things along.

While all of these conversational moves serve teachers' larger agendas of maintaining order and 'covering' a preset amount of material, they remain wholly rhetorical in their communicative purposes. Nevertheless, the pervasiveness of this speech sequence is prominent. The alternative to this familiar sequence is the concept of *conversation*, sequences between teacher and learners that represent active give and take negotiation of meaning.

As defined by Tharp and Gallimore, instructional conversations are those carefully calibrated and constructed things we say that comprise the essence of good teaching. These conversations can be initiated and guided by both learners and teachers who recognize and respond appropriately to the myriad teachable moments that present themselves in the course of human activity. To be successful instruction, the conversation involves several kinds of understandings: understanding the aims and purposes of the learning, understanding the learner(s), understanding the factors that constrain the conversation, understanding the importance of being open to multiple contingencies in the conversation, understanding what language would best bring about learner comprehension and action, and the like. It is a highly complex activity that we have all witnessed excellent teachers undertake facilely and effectively. As regards types or moves within instructional conversations, Tharp (1993) provides the following categories of assistance:

- Modeling.
- Feeding back.
- Contingency management.
- Instructing.
- Questioning.
- Cognitive structuring.
- Task structuring.

Further regarding these specific forms of assistance in learning processes, Tharp states that 'when the means of assistance are woven into the meaningful dialogue during joint activity, there exists the instructional conversation, the sine qua non of teaching' (Tharp, 1993: 273). In contrast to the tenacious IRE sequence, instructional conversations engage learners not in recitation of known answers (or punishment/remediation for unknown ones), but in thoughtful, engaging, communicative interaction. Learners thereby hone fluency in the social and intellectual practices of a given discipline.

In language education, professional educators step beyond these types of sequences in their quest to render their oral output comprehensible to learners, thereby assisting in learner comprehension and the potential for internalization or acquisition of certain features of the utterance or the utterance as a whole (Donato, 2000; Swain, 2007). Indeed, viewed as the primary meditational tools for second and foreign language development, instructional conversations serve simultaneously as language socialization for learners of additional languages. What renders the instructional conversation quintessentially *instructional* is the tailoring that a professional language educator undertakes to their side of the conversation. That tailoring involves aligning moment-by-moment learner comprehension and production using as a guide and touchstone the curricular trajectory they have set for groups and the individuals within.

Conversations focus on meaning primarily with the modeling, guiding, redirecting and authentic responding on the part of the teacher having its instructional objectives as structuring background. As Donato states, 'Instructional conversations are relevant to language classrooms because they socialize students into language learning in pragmatically rich contexts that facilitate language growth and development and provide opportunities for experiencing how language is used outside of the classroom' (Donato, 2000: 34).

What distinguishes a conversational move as *instructional*? First, there is instructional intention in the mind of the speaker or poster in online environments. This means that the instructor has in her mind a set trajectory along which she wishes to push the learning with goals and checkpoints along the way. Second, she has a sense of the current progress of an individual or group of learners along this trajectory. Gauging the current progress and rate of progress, she can appropriately design responses 'on the fly' that move the learning along successfully (Meskill, 2009).

For the field of language education, we can refine Tharp's list to include the following kinds of instructional conversation moves:

Calling attention to forms
Instructor (or a student) points out forms that a learner needs to be using.

Calling attention to lexis
Instructor (or a student) points out vocabulary words that a learner needs to be using.

Corralling
Instructor (or a student) redirects a learner's attention to specifics of language used.

Saturating
When a particular form (sets of vocabulary items and/or syntactic forms) is introduced and/ or reinforced, the instructor saturates the conversation with these focal forms.

Using linguistic traps
Instructor (or a student) traps a learner into using specific target language forms under study.

Modeling
Instructor (or a student) models forms for learners to appropriate and use.

Providing explicit feedback
Instructor (or a student) explicitly points out mistakes and remediates.

Providing implicit feedback
Instructor (or a student) implicitly indicates a mistake.

Indeed, in language education, the kinds of instructional conversation moves made on the part of excellent teachers are doubly complex in that they are instructional à la Tharp's definition, while being simultaneously *language* instruction, thus tailored and refined even more to the individual learning moment and event. In online environments, these socio-instructional moves carry particular potency where language learners can closely attend to instructional utterances and carefully compose their *instructed* responses. Teaching becomes running conversations to facilitate, synthesize, stir up opposing perspectives, play devil's advocate while drawing learners' attention to the very acts of instructional language use.

Conclusion

Engaging in instructional conversations in and of itself does not guarantee learning. It is the role of excellent language educators to craft tasks and accompanying responsive conversations so that opportunities for learning are optimized. Fully online and online portions of blended courses can be orchestrated as motivating communities where sociability and social processes constitute the forum for learning the new language. In such venues, learner development is focal and valued in every respect, not simply linguistic.

The special features of online environments can bring us to attend to our own dialogic, responsive practices with students, both online and in live classrooms. Given the time to draft and craft our conversations with students, we can use the medium to great advantage for language education. As we have seen, each of the four online environments offers a number of affordances that can support and enhance online instructional conversations: time to construct; time to think more carefully and complexly; time to compose questions and responses more thoughtfully; opportunities to recognize and respond to teachable moments; opportunities for evaluation to become part of the conversation with learners coming to be verified, acknowledged and valued beyond the 'That's right' evaluative turn of the IRE sequence. In the following chapters, additional affordances and instructional tools for teaching language well online will be discussed and illustrated.

References

Block, D. (2003) *The social turn in second language acquisition.* Washington DC: Georgetown University Press.

Chomsky, N. (1965) *Aspects of a theory of syntax.* Cambridge, MA: MIT Press.

Donato, R. (2000). Sociocultural contributions to understanding the foreign and second language classroom. In J. Lantolf (ed.) *Sociocultural theory and second language learning* (pp. 27–50). New York: Oxford University Press.

Goodwin, C. and Duranti, A. (1992) Rethinking context: An introduction. In Goodwin, C. and A. Duranti, (eds) *Rethinking context: Language as an interactive phenomenon* (pp. 191–227). New York: Cambridge University Press.

Foster, P. and Ohta, A. S. (2005) Negotiation for meaning and peer assistance in second language classrooms. *Applied Linguistics* 26, 402–430.

Hymes, D. (1971) *On communicative competence.* Philadelphia: University of Pennsylvania Press.

Hymes, D. (1972) Models of the interaction of language and social life. In J. Gumperz and D. Hymes (eds) *Directions in sociolinguistics* (pp. 35–71). New York: Hold, Rinehart & Winston.

Lantolf, J. (2000) *Sociocultural theory and second language learning.* New York: Oxford University Press.

Lantolf, J. and Pavlenko, A. (1995) Sociocultural theory and second language acquisition. *Annual Review of Applied Linguistics* 15 (1), 108–124.

Lantolf, J. and Poehner, M. (2008) Introduction: Sociocultural theory and the teaching of second languages. In J. Lantolf and M. Poehner (eds) *Sociocultural theory and the teaching of second languages.* London: Equinox.

Meskill, C. (2007) Producerly texts: Implications for language in education. *Journal of Language and Education* 21 (2), 95–106.

Meskill, C. (2009) Moment by moment formative assessment of English language learner development. In H. Adrande and G. Civek (eds) *Handbook of formative assessment*. New York: Routledge.

Meskill, C. and Anthony, N. (2007) Form-focused communicative practice via computer mediated communication: What language learners say. *Computer Assisted Language Instruction Consortium Journal* 25 (2), 69–90.

Savignon, S. J. (1983) *Communicative competence: Theory and classroom practice*. Reading, MA: Addison-Wesley.

Savignon, S. J. (1991) Communicative language teaching: State of the art. *TESOL Quarterly* 25 (2), 261–277.

Sinclair, J. and Coulthard, M. (1975) *Towards an analysis of discourse*. New York: Oxford University Press.

Swain, M. (2000) The output hypothesis and beyond: Mediating acquisition through collaborative dialog. In J. Lantolf (ed.) *Sociocultural theory and second language learning* (pp. 97–114). New York: Oxford University Press.

Swain, M. (2007) Languaging, agency and collaboration in advanced language proficiency. In H. Byrnes (ed.) *Advanced language learning: The contributions of Halliday and Vygotsky*. London: Continuum.

Tharp, R. (1993) Instruction and social context of educational practice and reform. In E. Forman, N. Minick and A. Stone (eds) *Contexts for learning: Sociocultural dynamics in children's development* (pp. 269–282). New York: Oxford University Press.

Tharp, R. and Gallimore, C. (1991) The instructional conversation: Teaching and learning as social activity. Research report 2, National Center for Research on Cultural Diversity and Second Language Learning. Retrieved July 12, 2004 from http://wee.ncela.gwu.edu/pubs/cnrcdsll/rr2.htm.

van Lier, L. (2000) From input to affordance: Social-interactive learning from an ecological perspective. In J. P. Lantolf, (ed.) *Sociocultural theory and second language learning* (pp. 245–260). Oxford: Oxford University Press.

Vygotsky, L. (1978) *Mind in society*. Cambridge, MA: Harvard University Press.

Zhang, J., Scardamalia, M., Lamon, M., Messina, R. and Reeve, R. (2007) Socio-cognitive dynamics of knowledge building in the work of nine- and ten-year-olds. *Educational Technology Research and Development* 55 (2), 117–145.

End of chapter activities

Activity A. Visual conventions

The fact that internet environments are generally constructed using set conventions with which most are familiar and comfortable means that little or no time is needed for learner orientation. Indeed, this familiarity can be viewed as a kind of foundation and scaffold for learning. Take a language textbook, for example. The more consistent the layout, the locations and character of the information, the more readily learners can make optimal use of the text. Have a look at some of the language learning sites available on the internet. Does their visual design make sense? Do the page designs conform to any inherent conventions? Which are the most intuitively appealing? Why?

Activity B. Ask yourself

Consider the various ways that you interact with others online. When do you consider this teaching? Learning? In what venues does this informal teaching and learning take place?

Share your observations with others.

Activity C. Language learning task development: chunquing[1]

Designing online language learning tasks and activities begins with the notion that useful material is comprised of real, not contrived or prescribed language. Historically, language instructors looked to 'the academy' or 'the queen' for a standard of language use for syllabus and materials design. Nowadays, it is the everyday discourse of the masses – how language is *actually used to get things done* by those who are *not* 'the queen' – that is the subject of study. Even though contemporary language textbooks aim towards authentic everyday culture and the discourse enacted within it, it remains the purview of the instructor to continually exercise their discourse analysis skills to determine the *what to teach* in language teaching.

'Chunquing'[2] is something very experienced language instructors do as a matter of course in their curricula and materials planning. Essentially, it is taking a broad view of language as it is used in real life target language contexts and selecting elements of that reality that make sense in combination. The resulting 'chunque' of language then becomes the targeted material that can be worked in any number of ways to teach the language. It is, in short, the essential building block in developing the kinds of language learning tasks you will encounter throughout this text.

Textbooks serve up ready-made chunques and accompanying activities. Experienced language instructors, especially those who are using online venues, are the first to say that this is not sufficient. Textbook materials often need 'rechunquing', reanalysis and expansion to be useful for a given population at a given point in a course, online or f2f. The central question is – given the infinite ways in which language is used in society, what system can a language task designer apply to create a tailored chunque for the focus of learning?

The **chunquing tool** is just such a system. It can guide you in attending to the anatomy of the language you teach, and in thinking through, designing and implementing mediated language learning tasks and activities. The system is by no means linear or simple. It requires that a number of considerations be attended to at the same time. Thoughtful construction of language chunques and the design of activities around them involve being a good eavesdropper. Listening critically and analytically to the target language as it is used around you is the fundamental basis for chunquing. Being aware of how the target language gets used, employing your linguistic and sociolinguistic competencies in determining appropriacy, and viewing language from the perspective of a non-native speaker – what queries or confusions might that learner have about how the language works – make up the chunquing process.

The first thing to understand about this tool is that there is no one right way to go about using it. It can be used to develop, supplement or enhance your materials in any way you see fit. Because we are dealing with teaching online, we can assume that the Chunquing Tool would be used to either repurpose existing materials (recorded sequences, digital learning objects, internet sites, etc.) or homemade materials. Either way, the place you begin to use this tool to think through your project is completely up to you. Though the skeleton below looks like it should be used linearly, it should not. Start anywhere. Revisit and revise each category as others evolve. Don't stop thinking, adding, deleting, expanding and contracting until you're happy with the chunque.

Here's what the tool looks like (Figure 4).

The Chunquing Tool

Learners: _____

Topic: _____

Situation: _____

Function(s): _____

Structure(s): _____

Lexis: _____

Skills foci: _____

Cultural notables: _____

Special expressions/idioms: _____

Medium/materials: _____

The chunque: _____

Figure 4 The chunquing tool

Here's a simple example of a 'from scratch' chunquing process:

You are midway through a 12-week term of teaching integrated skills to low-intermediate learners of ESL in a blended environment. Your course has been an eclectic, integrated combination of reading, writing and communicative work. Your learners are at a point where they are able to handle fairly sophisticated/abstract topics in their class activities. Their mastery of syntax in their speaking and writing is progressing and they respond well to challenges.

At this point, your students have difficulty making and responding to polite requests. You decide they could use some extra practice. You plug in *making polite requests* and *responding to polite requests* under *function* in the chunquing tool. You then consider the structures inherent in this activity (your eavesdropping and analytic skills are coming in handy now). You write down a couple of sample requests from your mental database – *Could you please... I would appreciate it if you... Do you think you might...* – and note that the past modal form is a common and, for your students, challenging structure. You fill in *past modals* under the structure heading. But, you realize that *making* this type of request is one thing; you had better include structures in appropriate ways of *responding*. Again you jot down samples from your internal dataset: *I'd be happy to, I'm afraid I can't.* But, wait a minute. Your learners are struggling with the appropriate negative replies to polite requests. You therefore decide to limit *responding to polite requests* to *responding to polite requests in the negative*. This will be sociolinguistically challenging given the complexity of this action in the target culture

Jump to *cultural notables.* Here you note that in the US it is imperative to 'soften' a negative response to a request, and that not doing so is perceived as very rude. You jump back up to *structures*: *I'm afraid I can't. I'd like to but + excuse. I'm terribly sorry, but + excuse.* Oh, yes, you say to yourself. The excuse. Back down to *cultural notables* where you make a note regarding the absolute requirement of some kind of excuse on the part of a speaker responding in the negative to a request. Back to *structures*. In generating a list of possible responses to requests, you notice that there are apologies of one sort or another built in to each. You also note that if your students are going to practice making excuses, these need to be made a part of your chunque. You add *apologizing* and *making excuses* to the *functions* heading and return to considering the structures inherent in these functions. You note that present modals and 'have to' are structures learners will use in politely refusing requests. You add these to the *structures* heading. You need to start limiting the context of these utterances so you begin brainstorming actual situations in which these utterances would naturally occur, and not only occur once, but many times as this will ultimately be the focus of learner activity/ practice with this language. You imagine a character who is requesting the unthinkable or the undoable of relative strangers. In what context, in what circumstances might this be authentic? What kind of request would elicit polite refusals accompanied, of course, by an apology? How might the excuse given for refusing be somewhat uniform across those being addressed by the request?

Although there are numerous situations that one can concoct for this linguistic transaction, you choose one you feel confident your students are familiar with, having most likely visited an airport at one time or another, and having followed the news regarding airport security regulations. They have, most likely, been asked by an airline employee, if they have at any time left their bags unattended, and whether someone asked them to put something in their luggage. The *situation* for the chunque, then, tentatively becomes someone in an airport approaching other passengers in the terminal and asking them to watch his/her luggage while she/he runs to the page phone.

As the situation begins to take shape, you review what you have already filled in regarding functions and structures and see you are on track. Next you start generating a tentative list of vocabulary items that may come into play. You fill these in under *lexis*: e.g. TSA agent, luggage, security, terrorism (terrorist, terrorize), prohibited, unsafe. Then you make a list of *special expressions*: against the rules/regulations, catch a plane, running late, ask a favor of, do someone a favor.

You started this chunque with functions, intending for learners to focus primarily on practicing sociolinguistic points, but see opportunities to integrate many more chunque elements as well. You see this as evolving into a chunque that is dense in linguistic, cultural and sociopolitical issues. You believe that you can get a lot of mileage out of the chunque by integrating skills foci as well by designing multiple activities each with emphasis on a linguistic aspect, skill, or issue. For example, in English when we make a polite request, there is a very formulaic pattern of intonation that looks something like this:

ExCUSE me (better add that in the function heading – *getting someone's attention*)

Could YOU please watch my LUGgage for a minute while I run to the page phone?

I'm SORry, I CAN't. I HAVE to CATCH my PLANE.

or

I'm SORry, but it's aGAINST AIRport reguLAtions.

You also note that the structures inherent in this chunque, the present and past modal forms, are structures that your learners would benefit a great deal from reviewing, especially the purposes these structures are put to in such situations. Focus and awareness of these, the functions outlined and the lexis you have begun to build will serve as the primary focus of the briefs, series of activities and debriefs for activities related to this chunque. Additionally, each activity will have one or more skills foci, like intonation in the case above.

A sample activity generated from this chunque is an extended role play cued by role play cards where one learner is given an A card and his/her partner a B card:

A: You are running to catch a plane when you're approached by a stranger.
 	
Use: I'm sorry, but ...
    It's against the rules to ...
	B: You're in a rush to catch your flight at the airport. Suddenly, you hear your name over the intercom. You're being paged and need to run to the page phone. Ask your partner to watch your bags.
	
	Use: Excuse me, but I'm in a rush
	    Could you please ...
	    I realize that, but ...

Cues like these can be given to learners as practice using the forms, functions and lexis in a more controlled communicative activity in either written or oral, synchronous or asynchronous forums. Likewise, more open-ended communicative practice can take place with simple cueing such as:

- A panel of airline customers making recommendations to airline security personnel.

- A scene where an airline check-in employee is told by a passenger that someone indeed handed them something to put in their bag or had offered to watch their bags while they were in the restroom.

- A scene where someone is stopped at the metal detector, searched, and nothing is found; or searched and a weapon is found.

Possibilities for expansion activities related to this chunque abound:

- going to the international airport security website and researching regulations;

- finding additional sites that discuss international terrorism at airports;

- locating news reports of air bombings.

All can be read, summarized, discussed and additional expansion activities can be built around them. To integrate writing practice, students can be asked to write about the situation you have designed or related topics (e.g. emails or letters to airline security officials commending their diligence; accounts to friends or family of their being asked to watch luggage and refusing; recommendations for passengers on how to behave in similar situations). While listening is part and parcel of the communicative activities – learners practice listening to one another during role plays, this can be made purposeful and form-focused. Specific listening activities can be designed by:

- locating or recording a sample/model conversation between native speakers and having learners isolate the forms and functions used;

- responding to a complete-the-dialogue orally or in writing;

- actively viewing airport video clips to compare the discourse to that of teacher- and/or class-generated discourse chunques.

A 'cultural notable' for a learner of ESL in the US would be that the simple excuse of *I'm sorry, but I'm in a hurry* would be a very common, non-confrontational response. Acceptable responses by country/culture will vary, and the issue of these differences is a prime opportunity for discussion whereby students can be chunquers themselves and report on what would work and not work in their native tongue/contexts. Another 'cultural notable' for ESL in the US would be the 'rush culture'; that is, being in a hurry is characteristic of many North Americans.

The extent to which you choose to employ the chunquing tool is always optional. Remember it is a tool to *think* with when designing and implementing language learning tasks generally and online language learning tasks in particular.

Now, give it a try. Select a real or fictitious group of language learners and determine a chunque of the target language they need work with. Use the chunquing tool to develop two or three tasks.

Notes

1. Adapted from Meskill (2009), *Teaching and learning in real time.*

2. The terms 'chunque' and 'chunquing' are used here in the context of social, integrative views of language teaching and learning. This spelling is used so as not to be confused with 'Chunking', Miller's (1956) cognitive strategy of breaking information into smaller units in order to facilitate memorization and recall.

2

Language learning and teaching in oral synchronous online environments

- Oral synchronous environments, their features and affordances, are presented.

- Illustrations and discussions of instructional conversations in these environments provide foundational understanding of how language learning and teaching are carried out in real time with voice.

- Methods of evaluating student learning are suggested.

- Issues involved in using translation and language teaching and learning in less formal environments are considered.

Language learning and teaching in oral synchronous online environments

Objectives:

In this chapter you will learn:

- the definition of oral synchronous online environments;

- the special affordances of oral synchronous online environments for language education;

- how different instructional conversation strategies can be undertaken in these environments;

- how the environment's affordances can be taken advantage of to support and amplify these conversations;

- methods for developing and applying language learning rubrics to align with task goals.

Oral synchronous online environments are one of the most promising instructional modes in online language education. Indeed, there is growing evidence that indicates that the environment's many affordances prove to be beneficial for developing learners' communicative skills in a target language (Levy & Kennedy, 2004; Wang, 2004, 2006). Audio/video conferencing in many ways resembles face-to-face (f2f), real-time classrooms by providing an environment whereby students can talk to each other and with their instructors using headsets or speakers and microphones with their personal computers. Most oral synchronous online environments offer the following functions: lists of participants, whiteboards for displaying and manipulating different documents, chat boxes, breakout rooms where an instructor can put students for small group activities, and application sharing features whereby instructors and students can display the content of their desktops. There are, as illustrated in Figure 5, a number of multimodal tools that can be used to amplify instructional conversation for language learning.

By manipulating uploaded files and electronic whiteboard tools, instructors can design and conduct activities emulating the f2f classroom's student–student and student–teacher interactions. In addition, oral synchronous online environment features not available in traditional classrooms, such as public and individual text messaging in the chat area, breakout rooms, web application sharing and recorded archives, can be very useful instructional tools. Archiving preserves not only the sounds but also all the movements performed on the whiteboard and in the chat area, such as typing or drawing foreign language characters and words, circling, underscoring, making notes, etc. so that what is spoken and typed is complemented in real time by any variety of visual supports. Figure 5 is an illustration of an instructor's interface in an oral synchronous online environment. The application is *Wimba Classroom*, one of many that are used in academic institutions.

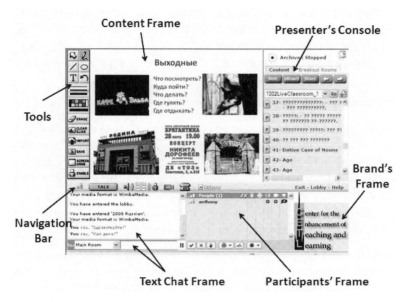

Figure 5 Oral synchronous online environment: instructor's interface

The affordances of oral synchronous online environments that distinguish this environment from the other three that we discuss is the incorporation of teacher and students' voices in real time while the teacher orchestrates visual information on the screen.

A central role of language educators is to make what learners hear and read in the target language understandable. By rendering the language comprehensible, teachers are in fact teaching the language, teaching learners what things mean and how the language works to make meaning. Language educators accomplish this in any number of creative ways, using any and all physical resources at hand. Online there are, of course, unlimited resources, all of which are not only accessible but can be both manipulated and archived and thus returned to and referred to instantaneously and repeatedly as needed as part of the flow of instructional conversations. These resources can be images (still, video or animations), textual information and sounds.

Unlike the subsequent online environments we examine in later chapters, teachers in synchronous oral environments can enjoy using tools that address all learning modalities, including their voices. Like in the live language classroom, when it comes to rendering challenging target language comprehensible to learners, these multiple modalities can be used to great effect. In the following sections, we discuss and illustrate how this orchestration happens while focusing on the instructional conversations that generate language instruction.

Calling attention to forms

Much like the live classroom, oral synchronous online environments offer similar visual, aural and action-oriented tools to draw learners' attention to the particular forms under study during authentic task-based exchanges. Learners listen to the instructor's and their classmates' voices while viewing visual information that complements and anchors the meaning-focus of the oral/aural and optional text communication. And, as is the case in the live classroom, learners can take action based on what they understand or don't understand.

Task-level attention to form

Tasks can be assigned to individuals, pairs or groups of students much as they can be assigned in the live classroom. The form(s) and/or lexical items on which learners are to focus during the task can be made prominently known via text, icon and/or diagram. A consistent location on the screen for this instructional objective information is a must. We call this a **task toolkit**. This way, both learners and instructor can simply point to, or highlight key linguistic information when attention needs to be drawn to it; e.g. if learners stray from the target forms in unproductive ways, or there is an error or gap in learner output.

In the following example, English-speaking learners of Japanese are practicing different ways of communicating with one another by role playing different pairs of native Japanese while assigned to breakout rooms. Each pair has the same **task toolkit** on their screens (Figure 6) which, in this case consists of a concise guide to the humble, honorific and polite forms of address. The information in the **task toolkit** serves as an anchor to keep student attention focused on the focal forms while they are practicing the use of these forms in different situations simulating real life.

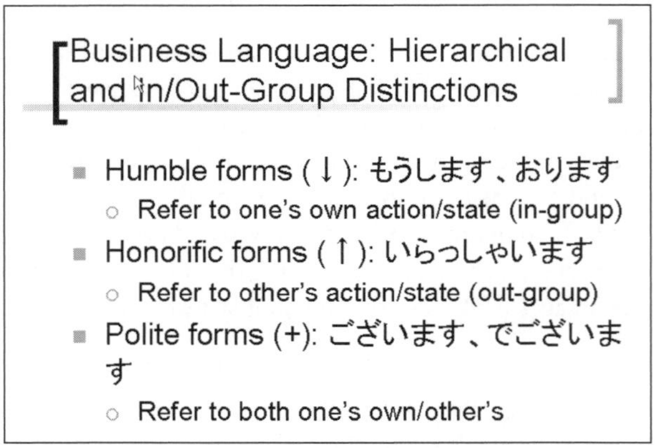

> **Business Language: Hierarchical and In/Out-Group Distinctions**
>
> - Humble forms (↓): もうします、おります
>   - Refer to one's own action/state (in-group)
> - Honorific forms (↑): いらっしゃいます
>   - Refer to other's action/state (out-group)
> - Polite forms (+): ございます、でございます
>   - Refer to both one's own/other's

Figure 6 Task toolkit for Japanese honorifics

The more sophisticated new audio conferencing technologies become, the more opportunities they provide for task-level attention to form whereby visual representations of rules can be continuously incorporated into communicative streams as tools to guide, remind, direct, and serve to reinforce the form as it is used. In this example, Russian learners are prompted to answer the questions: Do you often go to New York? Do you often go to Russia? Where do you go often? Where did you go in August? Where did you go last summer? Do you like to ride in cars? Do you ride a motorcycle well? Do you like to drive around the city? All these questions are displayed on the primary screen. With the help of the application sharing feature, the instructor opens a new window displaying a

Word document file with the visual representations of the four situations in which a certain form of a verb 'to go', a multidirectional form, would be used: habitual movement, round trips in the past, random movement, and preferences/qualities of the movement (Figure 7). The small screen also provides a model of use for this verb in the first person singular form, the one that students are most likely to use when answering these questions. This type of task-level attention to form is supported by multi-pane views of internet sites and TV news.

Figure 7 Textual/iconic task-level attention to form

Often instructors use the same screen to display the task/activity explanation and directions as well as the **task toolkit** to assist learners with their task. In the next example, pairs of Russian learners can simultaneously speak to and Instant Message (IM) one another while they accomplish the assigned task of planning a trip abroad with the specific goal of choosing the best country for traveling (Figure 8). The focal forms are the ways in which suggestions are made and accepted or rejected.

This core information – the **task toolkit** – is displayed in the upper right-hand corner of the screen with links to elaborations on use, usage, and additional contexts of use for these forms so that students can constantly refer to them while performing the task (Figure 9). Prior to the pair tasking conversations, the instructor models (1) the pronunciation and intonation of these forms; and (2) how to point to this instructional objectives information – the **task toolkit** – during the task both when assisting a partner and producing the language oneself as part of the task. As the instructor monitors individual pairs while they undertake the task, they too can point to the **task toolkit** in the corner of the screen to remind learners of the activity focus/the linguistic objectives while not interrupting the flow of authentic communication practice in the target language. As shown in Figure 8, the instructor can easily call additional attention to these forms by using such whiteboard functions as drawing and making arrows. As task synthesis, pairs can report back both the meaning content of their work as well as the linguistic object content of their work again by referring to the key information in the upper right-hand corner of the screen.

Figure 8 Textual task-level attention to form

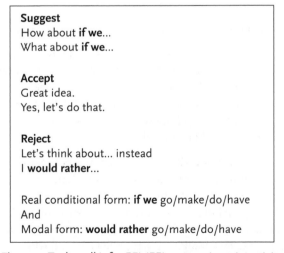

Figure 9 Task toolkit for EFL/EFL suggesting trip activity

In the following example, we see how the **task toolkit** is referred to by learners themselves in this mid-beginning Spanish class whose small group task it is to direct the movements of screen avatars using the imperative form of the verb. In their **task toolkit** (Figure 10) they see:

T: Dígale el amigo cómo mover al avatar. [Tell your partner to move his avatar..]

sobre el suyo [above yours]
debajo el suyo [below yours]
a la derecha el suyo [to the right of yours]
a la izquierda el suyo [to the left of yours]

Una vez que usted tiene la forma correcta, tome una fotografía. Entonces, demuestre la fotografía a la clase con el diálogo correspondiente. [Once you have the correct form, take a picture. Then, show your picture to the class with the corresponding dialog.]

el imperativo	
-ar verbs	
tu	-a
el, ella, usted	-e
nosotros, tras	-emos
vosotros, tras	-ad
ustedes	-en
> -ir	
> -er	

In another window (Figure 10) they are in Second Life where each pair has their own avatar active on the screen. As they give commands to one another to move the avatars into the indicated configurations, two additional declensions for -er and -ir verbs can be turned to as well. As the pairs work independently to accomplish the task, the instructor monitors and calls attention to uses of the imperative and prepositional phrases as needed. During the whole class review of the pair photographs plus dialogs, students themselves can make use of referring to the task toolkit's elements as needed.

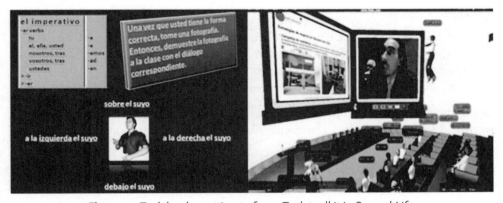

Figure 10 Task-level attention to form. Task toolkit in Second Life

Incidental attention to forms

While students are communicating with the instructor and learners with one another in various configurations for any number of authentic and orchestrated purposes, there is ample opportunity, any number of teachable moments whereby learners' attention can be drawn to form(s) via: circling, underscoring, arrows, wiping clean, crossing out, writing (e.g. particles, morphological pieces), check marking, drawing, bracketing, etc.

Indeed, attention to form can be called in ways similar to those of the traditional classroom as in the following example. Here, students are provided different photographs and are asked to play detective: to tell as much about the people in the photos as they can, trying to figure out their occupations and nationalities. In this example one of the students becomes confused about the use of two different forms, 'Russian' as a noun and 'Russian' as an adjective, each having different endings in the Russian language. The instructor explicitly explains the difference and, after several turns, calls students' attention to the same linguistic concept, using a different word, 'American', as a noun and as an adjective. Simultaneously, the teacher uses her voice to draw attention and to emphasize the salient similarities and differences in linguistic forms.

T: Как его зовут? [What is his name?]

S: Его зовут доктор Пол Гейтс. [His name is Dr. Paul Gates.]

T: Кто такой доктор Пол Гейтс? [What is Dr. Paul Gates?]

S: Он профессор. [He is a professor.]

T: Он русский профессор? [Is he a Russian professor?]

S: Нет, он американский   американец. (No, he is an American... American...) How's that, I'm sorry. Он американец or ... [He's American or...]

T: If you say "He is an American professor" then American is an adjective – американский [American]. And if you say "He is American" then American is a noun – американец [American] (*American as a noun and American as an adjective have slightly different forms*).

S: OK, all right.

(After several turns, the instructor decides to reinforce the form incidentally as a part of a meaningful conversation)

T: Его зовут Ричард Гир. Он русский? [His name is Richard Gere. Is he Russian?]

S: Нет, он американец. [No, he's American.]

T: Он русский актер? [Is he a Russian actor?]

S: Нет, он американский актер. [No, he is an American actor.]

Calling attention to form can be amplified via additional visual emphasis. In the next example, the instructor circles as an intensifying gesture calling attention to the linguistic form (Figure 11).

T: Где они? [Where are they?]

S: Они на школе. [They are on (*wrong preposition*) school.]

T: (*switches the slide and returns to the grammar explanation; underscores the form "в школе" [at school] as in Figure 11*)

S: (*silence for 11 seconds*)

T: (*circles the linguistic form as in Figure 11*)

S: Они в школе. [They are at (*correct preposition*) school.]

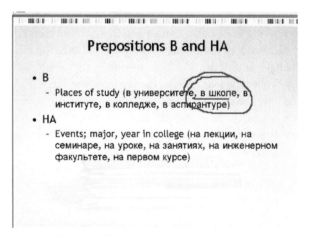

Figure 11 Visual reinforcement of incidental attention to form

Calling attention to lexis

In authentic meaning negotiation, comprehending and using lexical items appropriately in a new language is challenging. In oral synchronous environments there are numerous resources and tools – aural, visual, textual and action-oriented – that instructors can make productive use of to call attention to lexical items and their corresponding meaning. These features, when used thoughtfully, can be viewed as visually enriching and, therefore, enriching the acquisition experiences of learners.

Task-level attention to lexis

Tasks that focus learner attention on comprehending and producing specific lexical items during authentic communication practice can be generated from the syllabus, core text or based on students' instructional needs and/or personal interests. The fact of infinite visual resources freely available online along with ready translations, digital pronunciation and authentic, contextualized uses of target lexical items makes drawing attention to the connection between spoken/written words and their meanings a richly enhanced proposition. And, like calling attention to form(s), calling attention to lexical items for comprehension or production can happen on the fly, in real time by manipulating what is on the screen and thereby avoid interrupting the natural flow of meaningful interaction.

In this ESL/EFL example, students have been studying vocabulary associated with global warming. Here as a group they are discussing actions that they can take as individuals and as members of their communities to halt negative climate change. In the upper right corner of the screen, a word bank containing lexical items typically occurring in discourse concerning global warming has been created, and students and their instructor have cached a number of key vocabulary words there to reference during this and subsequent learning activities that are related to this theme (Figure 12). Note: the list will become part of a larger vocabulary bank that is being built in the course and that can be referenced throughout. The instructor has asked each student to formulate and pose a discussion question. They can, of course, make use of whatever online and offline resources they wish. As they pose and respond to their online colleagues' questions, the students use the word bank and its links to visuals and extended meanings to comprehend and produce utterances in the target language. When there is a gap or error in word use, the instructor and/or other students use the word bank to point this out without breaking up the flow of conversation. They can, when the discussion is over, access the recording of their discussion accompanied by the visual tracking of screen activity for review. Using these same records, the instructor can construct future assignments based on the strengths and weaknesses of the language comprehension and performance thus documented.

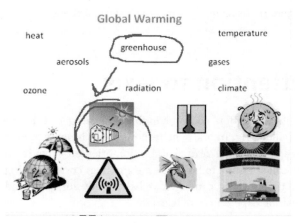

Figure 12 Task-level attention to lexis

Calling attention to lexis in oral synchronous online environments can occur in ways similar to how this happens in a f2f classroom. In meaning negotiation, students simply ask how to say this or that word in the target language. Instructors can provide lexical forms immediately when students request these. Alternately, students can be prompted and encouraged to search for the lexical item on their own. In this example, the student asks how to say 'fun' in Russian. The instructor does not answer right away but in a playful manner prompts students to make guesses, and provides a translation only after attempts to find synonyms fail.

S1: Что мы делаем весной? [What do we do in spring?]
S2: Мы катаемся на рафтах. [We raft.]
T: Ты правда катаешься на рафтах? [Do you indeed raft?]
S2: Один раз. Да. [One time. Yes.]
T: Ты не боишься? [Aren't you afraid?]
S2: Нет, мне очень нравится. [No, I like it very much.]
T: Я никогда не каталась на рафтах, но очень хочу. [I have never done rafting but I want to very much.]

S2:   Очень [Very] fun. Wait, how to say "fun"? (*laughing*)

T: Я не знаю, как сказать "fun." Это английское слово. [I don't know how to say "fun." It's an English word.]

S3:   Интересно? [Interesting?]

S1:   Хорошо? [Good?]

T: Весело. [Fun.]

S2:   Очень весело. [Very much fun.]

Calling attention to lexis in oral synchronous online environments can be done on the fly by using the range of multimodal resources immediately available. Internet sources such as web encyclopedias, informational sites, online dictionaries, search engines, etc. can all be accessed by instructors and by students to supply and reinforce the lexical items. In the following example, a student asks what the word 'велосипед' [bicycle] means, and the instructor, using the application sharing feature, immediately sends an image to students, having googled the image of a bicycle. This is an enormous advantage of online synchronous teaching. All the possible sources are right at the instructor's fingertips.

T: Энн, ты любишь ездить на велосипеде? [Ann, do you like to ride a bicycle?]

S: Я не знаю, что «велосипед» значит. [I don't know what "velosiped" means.]

T: I'll show it to you through the Application Sharing. (*turns on the application sharing feature, opens another window on her desktop, goes to the Google web site, types in "велосипед" [bicycle] into the search box; the page with the image appears on the screen*) Это велосипед. А это красные велосипеды. Много велосипедов. Энн, ты любишь ездить на велосипеде? [This is a bicycle. These are red bicycles. Many bicycles. Ann, do you like to ride a bicycle?]

Incidental attention to lexis

Gaps and misunderstandings around lexical items happen frequently in conversations using the target language. Like drawing learner attention to form(s) while they are engaged in activities that do not have those forms as their underlying linguistic objectives, instructors and learners can take advantage of the tools and resources at hand to support attention to, and connectivity of, lexical items and their meanings.

T: Умница. Очень хорошо [Good girl. Very good]. Do you know the meaning of the word "умница" ["good girl"]?

S: Нет [No].

T: УМНИЦА [SMARTY] means smarty. (*draws the word on the whiteboard while pronouncing it slowly with an emphasis*) (Figure 13)

These real-time voice-plus-visual strategies for drawing learners' attention to vocabulary items take advantage of the aural (teacher stress and intonation) and the visual (circling the image to which the lexical item corresponds). The synchronous aspect requires that both instructor and students attend carefully to the moment-by-moment unfolding of their conversations as well as to aspects of written and spoken production and comprehension whereby lexical learning and reinforcement are possible.

**Accusative Case -
Meaning**

- Direct Object
  - Maria studies business.
  - Anthony is reading a newspaper.
  - Brian is watching TV.
  - We understand Russian well.
  - Anna likes Latin.

УМНИЦа

Figure 13 Incidental attention to lexis

Corralling

A key part of language instruction is providing effective cues and guidance so that learners can both understand and produce the portions of the language that the instructor intends; in short to orchestrate practice with the target language that is narrowly focused on their instructional objectives at the moment. A strategy that accomplishes this goal is corralling; by analogy, rounding up learners' attention into a specific corner of the corral so that their attention is finely focused on what language should be attended to and learned. It is a common strategy in f2f settings as students can stray from the instructional path the instructor has in mind. Even when learners are 'on track', it is the instructor who directs them to go on comprehending and producing the language of her instructional objectives.

Task-level corralling

When there are carefully designed language objectives behind well-designed tasks, corralling may still remain in order. Students, after all, do not always follow predictable paths in what they do and say. A group task whereby members are all equally involved in accomplishing a common goal needs instructor support to move it along but also to redirect and refocus learners' attention to the featured forms or lexical items or phonemes that are the educational purpose of the task. In this task, a group of English learners has been directed to design a website for a class member's new online business. As a group they have brainstormed forms and lexical items germane to both the new business (electronic business card design and production) and to the process of designing a website. Some of the language the group suggests in the process is not appropriate to either and digressions about language irrelevant to the task begin.

S1:   And, you know, we can make nice letters like card...
S2:   Font, you mean?
S1:   Fountain? You mean like fountain?
S3:   In church. Yes, font for washing.
T: You mean the shape of the letters, the font, correct?
S1:   Yes. Font. We can make nice font on the page like card.
T: Yes, font. Can you all repeat: fOnt (*emphasizing vowel sound*)

Learners are thus corralled into the appropriate meaning, and later for appropriate use, for a key word they will need to use in their discussion. Later, once the group has generated a list of focal forms and lexical items to go into the **task toolkit** in the upper right-hand corner of the screen, this information becomes available to reference throughout the actual task of designing a website for a student in the class.

Incidental corralling

As we all know, tasks of all kinds are subject to meandering digressions. In language education contexts, however, all of these can be viewed as teachable moments by the attentive educator. Take, for example, learners veering off track and thereby avoiding use of the focal syntactic or lexical forms of the assigned task. In this example, the task is to report events from the past weekend using the past progressive (*was/were –ing*) plus *when* plus the *past tense*; e.g. I was watching television when the phone rang. As learners take turns reporting while their partners type in the chat box what they hear, the instructor monitors their uses of this syntactic form as well as their use of lexical items from the list provided as part of the task. She hears the following and sees the partner's written version:

S1:   The sun shine yesterday and I go park.
T: (*voice plus text with tenses highlighted*) The sun was ---?? yesterday?
S1:   Sun was shining..
T: When you --- to the park?
S1:   When I went to the park.
T: So, when you went to the park, the sun was shining?
S1:   The sun was shining when I went to the park.
S2   (*typing in correct sentence*) The sun was shining when he went to the park.
T: And what was ---ing?
S2:   And, what was going on when you arrived at the park?

Both partners are thereby corralled into producing, both in speech and writing, the correct form of their utterances with the aid of live speech and synchronous written messages. In this way the instructional conversation is fully supported by the affordances of the synchronous aural environment.

Instructors often make attempts to elicit target forms from students as a form of practice. In trying to elicit certain forms, instructors often provoke numerous guesses from students which leads to an authentic conversation involving the active use of different words and constructions in the context of a meaningful conversation. In the following example, the instructor tries to elicit the verb 'to tan' from the student by asking what people do on a beach. However, the student, who is not a fan of tanning, makes several guesses, suggesting other possible activities which she preferred to do on a beach. In doing so, she uses verbs from the list of active vocabulary in the **task toolkit** and from those of previous lessons, such as 'to sleep' and 'to read'. She also uses the word 'accidentally', not on the vocabulary list for this course, which she knew from other sources. The situation is perfect for prompting her to use those otherwise non-active vocabulary items. A visual representation of the target lexical item is finally provided to avoid translation and to direct the student to using the target form.

S1:   Что они делают летом? [What do they do in summer?]

S2:   Они лежат на пляже. [They are lying down on the beach.]

T: Да, они лежат на пляже. И что они делают на пляже? Лежат и? [Yes, they are lying down on the beach. And what are they doing on the beach? Lying down and?]

S2:   Спят. Спят? [Sleeping. Sleeping?]

T: (*laughing*) Нет, они не спят. [No, they are not sleeping.]

S2:   Я спю. [I sleep.]

T: Ты спишь? [Do you sleep?]

S2:   Да. На пляже летом. [Yes. On a beach in summer.]

T: А ты загораешь? [Do you tan?]

S2:   Загораешь? [Tan?]

T: (*draws a sun with the beams*) (Figure 14)

S2:   Yeah.. Нечаянно. [Accidentally.]

T: А, случайно загораешь? [Oh, get tanned by chance?]

S2:   Да. Иногда загораешь... загораю. Но я люблю спать больше. И читать на пляже. [Yes. Sometimes I tans... tan. But I like to sleep more. And read on a beach.]

Figure 14 Visual attention to lexis

Instructional conversations whereby such forms of incidental attention to lexis can be commonplace teaching strategies in oral synchronous online environments.

Saturating

In live language learning contexts, repetition of the target words and forms are standard fare. It is, after all, by hearing, using, reading and, in general, encountering the target language over and over that learning is facilitated. Language learners often use repetition on their own to reinforce remembering the sound, look and feel of new forms. The instructional conversation technique of saturation differs from simply repeating because what gets repeated happens in authentic conversational contexts. Rather than simply saying or writing what an instructor wants learners to attend to and internalize, they can use the target within a meaningful context repeatedly. Take the following example. EFL learners are discussing their hobbies. It is clear that three of the lexical items in the **task toolkit** list are unknown to them. Realizing that these are new vocabulary items, the instructor uses them as frequently as possible in her spoken and written utterances.

T: Yes, in the US **biking** is a popular hobby. People go **biking** all the time. Some go **biking** for exercise, some go **biking** to be outside in good weather. Families often go **biking** as a family activity.

In turn, the instructor can employ corralling techniques to guide learners in producing utterances with the target words as well as a means of reinforcing attention to the new term.

As the class **task toolkit** expands with new words and new forms, it can be continually referred to by both students and instructor. Students themselves can be encouraged to use saturation as well as a means of reinforcing their own mastery of new words and forms and also as a way to play an instructional role in the class's instructional conversations.

In oral synchronous online environments, saturating can be accomplished in several modes simultaneously. Instructors can inject the target forms into their oral production and at the same time call attention to those, using non-verbal clues as in this example.

T: When we talk about playing sports and playing musical instruments, we use the same verb "ИГРАТЬ" [TO PLAY] in both constructions, right? (*underscores the verbs "ИГРАТЬ" [TO PLAY] in two places as in Figure 15*). But we use different prepositions and different cases in these constructions. (*wipes everything away*) You have to remember when you talk about playing sports, after "ИГРАТЬ" [TO PLAY] (*underscores "ИГРАТЬ" [TO PLAY]*) you use "в" [in] (*underscores "в" [in]*) and then Accusative forms (*underscores the word "Accusative" as in Figure 16*) of sports. (*wipes everything away*) The nouns for sports are masculine. So, in Accusative case you don't change them. Don't add any endings. ИГРАТЬ в гольф, ИГРАТЬ в теннис, ИГРАТЬ в баскетбол, ИГРАТЬ в воллейбол... [TO PLAY golf, TO PLAY tennis, TO PLAY basketball, TO PLAY volleyball...] (*as she names the sport activities, she underscores them as in Figure 17*) When we talk about playing musical instruments, we use "на" [on] (*underscores "на" [on]*) and then the Prepositional case which has the ending "е" [e] (*underscores the endings of all the nouns*). ИГРАТЬ на скрипке, ИГРАТЬ на рояле, ИГРАТЬ на гитаре, ИГРАТЬ на барабане... [TO PLAY violin, TO PLAY piano, TO

PLAY guitar, TO PLAY drum...] (*as she names the musical instruments, she underscores them as in Figure 17*)

These visual gestures calling attention to forms while saturating the discourse with those forms are instrumental in riveting students' attention to them in real time.

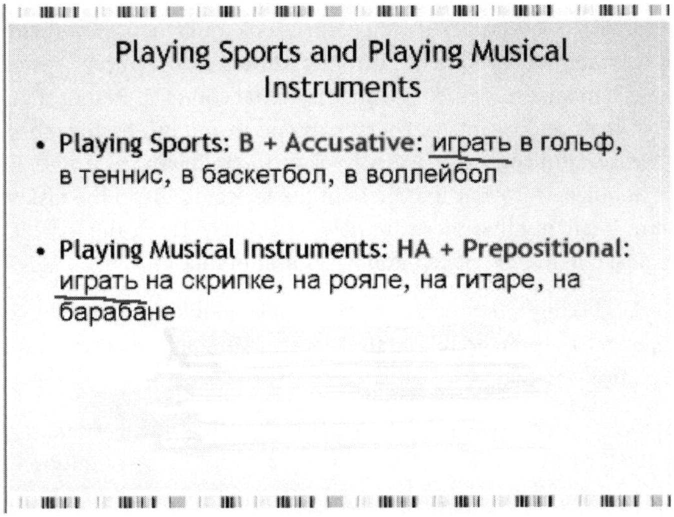

Figure 15 Visual saturating

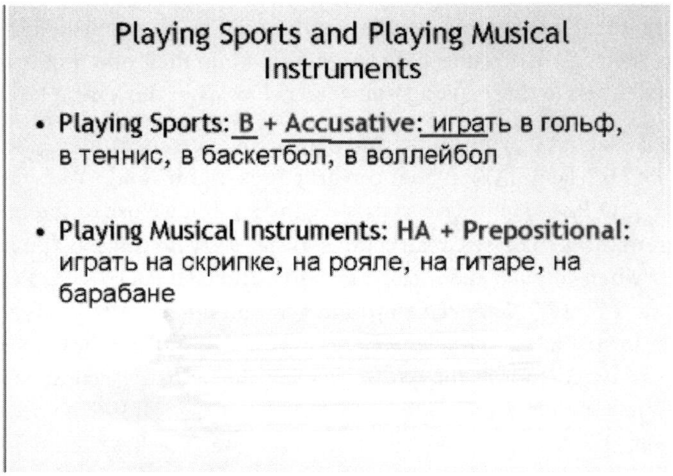

Figure 16 Visual saturating

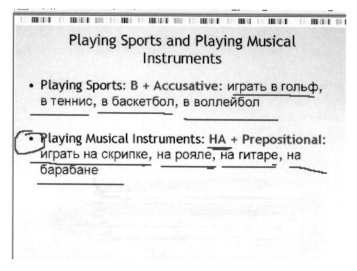

Figure 17 Visual saturating

Using linguistic traps

We realize that 'trapping' students may have negative connotations, but we felt it was a better term than 'tricking'. We use the word 'trap' to mean that learners have no choice but to use the linguistic target we have in mind. Say, for example, an instructor is orchestrating a whole class task with the main focus being on comprehension and use of gerunds (-ing forms of verbs that serve as nouns in special contexts). Her secondary objective is intonation. The task is designed so that learners share things that their friends or family members do that they find annoying. The teacher models how to use the target form including using her voice to model the intonation for complaints and commiserating by saying 'My *mother* likes to *hum*. Her *hum*ming drives me *crazy*. What drives *you* crazy?' Students in turn cue one another by asking the question: What drives *you* crazy? When students hesitate, falter or use an incorrect form, the teacher employs linguistic traps such as the following.

T: So, your brother plays the drums. Does his drumming drive you crazy?
S: Yes. Crazy.
T: His drumming –
S: His drumming drive
T: His drumming drives
S: His drumming drives me crazy.
S: His drumming drives me crazy.
T: His *drum*ming drives me *crazy*.
S: His *drum*ming drives me *crazy*.
T: I can see why. *Drum*ming drives *me* crazy *too*!

In the next example, the instructor traps Russian learners into using the verb *play* using non-verbal means.

T: Что они делают? [What are they doing?] (*circles the images of two baseball players as in Figure 18*)

S: Они в бейсбол. [They baseball] (*misses the verb "to play"*)

T: Right but what are they doing? How do we say "playing"? [*underscores the word "playing" on the slide as in Figure 18*]

S: Они играют в бейсбол. [They play baseball.]

Figure 18 Non-verbal linguistic trap

In the next example, students are asked to tell what they did during a certain period of the day. One student says 'в три часа' [at 3 o'clock] but does not specify the time of the day by adding the word 'вечера' [PM]. The instructor silently underscores 'PM' on the slide pointing out to the student that he needs to be more specific thus visually trapping the student to employ the correct form.

S1:   Во сколько вы играете в теннис? [At what time do you play tennis?]

S2:   Я играю в теннис в три часа. [I play tennis at 3 o'clock.]

T: (*underscores "PM" on the slide as in Figure 19*)

S2:   Я играю в теннис в три часа дня. [I play tennis at 3 o'clock in the afternoon.]

Such 'traps' are in effect guides to learner productions and support their searching for and supplying the focal pieces of the target utterance. This kind of guidance can be employed to great effect in synchronous oral online environments where the traps can be set by the teacher's voice, accompanying image, text or action of what she is saying, and pointing and referring to the correct form in the **task toolkit**.

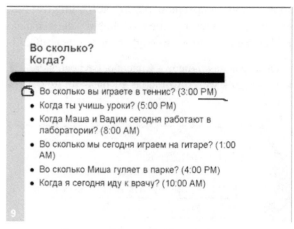

Figure 19 Non-verbal linguistic trap

Modeling

Clearly, any task we assign learners must be made comprehensible to them so that they can succeed in undertaking it. The most straightforward way to assist learners in understanding what it is they are to do is by modeling. For example, stress and intonation are exquisite tools for drawing learner attention to an aspect or aspects of what they hear, read, or are producing. In oral synchronous environments this modeling can be done in any one or combination of modalities. For example, if the task involves learners using correct intonation contours in making requests, instructors can assist by

-modeling the target intonation pattern with their voice:
-plus line diagram
-plus in-text emphasis (caps, bold, italics, font size)
-plus animated spectrograph
-plus video clips of native speakers doing same

In this example, an EFL instructor models the US intonation pattern of accepting a gift. The target pattern is:

You SHOULDn't have.

As she models the intonation pattern with her voice, she draws an accompanying intonation contour line above the text version of her utterance. Then, she plays the spectrograph of her output as well as two video clips (labeled 'At a Birthday Party' and 'On Valentine's Day') of native speakers in authentic situations using this pattern conversationally, thereby culturally situating the focal language.

In this example, double underscoring is used to focus students on new words useful to the task at hand: invitations to different places. The instructor wants to introduce the phrase for answering the invitation – 'С удовольствием' [I'd love to!/With great pleasure]. The instructor underscores this phrase twice while modeling its use in a dialog. She also slows down her pace and makes the intonation stressed as the word is difficult to pronounce.

T: - Я хочу пригласить тебя на концерт. - Спасибо. С удовольствием. [- I want to invite you to the concert. - Thank you. It would be my pleasure (to go).] (*underscores the last phrase as in Figure 20*)

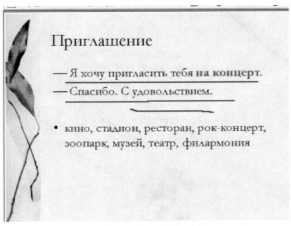

Figure 20 Visual models

In this example, a Japanese instructor repeatedly models the use of a common expression highlighting it on the screen.

T: This expression "so deskhaa" (*highlights the Japanese word as in Figure 21*) is used to disagree with someone. Are you sure? Really? Is that so? Using a long vowel standard pronunciation "xaa" with the raising intonation. So deskhaa? Right? Are you sure? So deskhaa? OK.

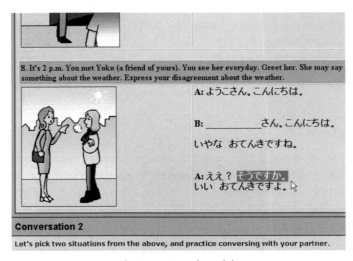

Figure 21 Visual models

Providing explicit feedback

A good deal of language teaching involves explaining the quirks and mechanics of the target language to students as they learn these. Common to such explanations is the use of metalanguage, or language about language. Research indicates that learners beyond childhood generally respond well to such explanations as they are equipped with the higher cognitive skills and abilities to both comprehend and internalize patterns and their rules. The judicious use of explicit language about the targets under study is indeed an important pedagogical tool. What, then, do we do with explicit forms of feedback in online teaching? As with the other instructional conversation strategies we have discussed, we make use of explicit feedback by using the modalities the oral synchronous environment affords.

    Referring to the relevant rule in the **toolkit**
    Pointing to a visual representation
    Pointing to a rule in text form
    Speaking/writing the rule (having another student do the same)

Corrective feedback in oral synchronous online environments is often transformed into explicit non-verbal indications of errors in students' utterances. Such indicative moves as *silently* marking the slide with underscoring, circling or drawing emoticons/icons/metaphors, *silently* returning to the slides with explicit grammar explanations or models, and *silently* writing down on the slide or typing correct forms in the chat box are common instructional conversation strategies in oral synchronous online environments. These moves allow for an economical use of time and a friendlier and even more playful environment for learning.

 The instructor of an intermediate Russian class provides negative explicit feedback with the use of visual metalanguage.

T: (*showing the slide with the images of people; Figure 22*) Tell me if these clothes look nice or not so nice on these people (*circles the name Вера [Vera]*).

S: Вера... [Vera... (*incorrect ending*)]

T: (*underscores the ending in "Vera"*)

S: Вере [Vera (*correct ending*)].

T: (*draws a smiley face*)

S: Идут платье... [Dress look (*erroneously used the plural ending instead of the singular ending*) good on...].

T: (*circles the dress, writes the digit 1 next to it, underscores the verbs "идём/идут" [looks nice/ look nice], and draws a question mark*).

Figure 22 Providing visual explicit feedback

Student: Oh, it's идёт [looks nice].

Explicit feedback in the above example is provided silently. The instructor manipulates the slide, provides hints and clues, and avoids the use of dense metalanguage and grammatical terms. Yet, students are able to figure out their problems and correct themselves. Silent visual explicit feedback is effective for students of different language competency levels and minimizes the interruption of conversational flow. Metalanguage as explicit feedback can thereby be replaced by its iconic or metaphoric representations as in these examples.

In this drill and practice assignment, students are asked to change the adjectives and nouns in parentheses, putting them into the accusative forms.

S: Ты понимаешь новый профессор? [Do you understand the new professor?] (*incorrect Accusative case endings for masculine animate nouns and modifiers*)

T: (*draws a male figure to hint to the gender of the noun and modifiers and a sad face as in Figure 23*)

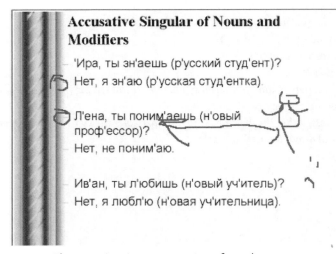

Figure 23 Iconic representation of metalanguage

In another example, the instructor draws a house pointing out the difference between the use of the prepositions В [in] and НА [on]. В [in] is mostly used in talking about enclosed spaces such as buildings, rooms, apartments, etc. as opposed to open spaces such as streets, stadiums, etc.

S: Я хочу пригласить тебя на музей. [I want to invite you on (*wrong preposition*) the museum.]

T: (*underscores the word museum and draws a house, referring to the idea of a museum being a building, not an event or an open space as in Figure 24*)

S: (*laughing*) Я хочу пригласить тебя в музей. [I want to invite you to (*correct preposition*) the museum.]

T: (*draws the preposition В [in]*)

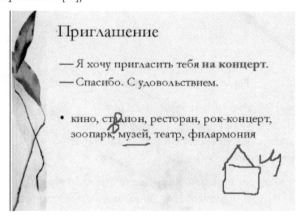

Figure 24 Metaphoric representation of metalanguage

Form-focused feedback can be provided in a non-intrusive yet effective way by utilizing the overhead projector technique (writing on slides). Students are engaged in a drill and practice activity, asking each other 'What is it?' with the purpose of practicing how to use the word 'and'. The instructor reacts to an error in the student's utterance by drawing a missing word on the slide.

S1:   Что это? [What is it?]

S2:   Это письмо книга. [This is a letter a book.]

T: (*draws "И" [and] in between the two pictures; Figure 25*)

S2:   Это письмо и книга. [This is a letter and a book.] (*corrects herself*)

With text messaging features explicit feedback can be much less intrusive than in a traditional classroom. Students often become engaged in meaningful conversations by simply switching to the text-based mode while instructors take a break on focusing on focal forms. Combined with non-verbal focus on form by the instructor, this switch to another mode helps the conversation continue and minimizes the effects of interruptions. It should be noted that continuation of conversations through the chat box can be playful. Students can find it safe and fun to continue a conversation in a humorous way without any specific instructional constraints.

Что 'это?

Figure 25 Non-verbal explicit feedback

S1:   Ты в чём сейчас? [What do you have on right now?]
S2:   Я в джинсах. [I'm in jeans.]
S1:   Какого цвета твои джинсы? [What color are your jeans?]
S2:   Зелёный. [Green. (*erroneous ending*)]

(*simultaneously*)   T: (*circles the adjectival ending in the model provided*)
                        S1:   (*types in the chat box*) Ооооо почему??? Я хочу знать, почему! Пожалуйста, почемууууу? [Ohh why??? I want to know why! Please whhhhhhy?]

Sometimes students become engaged in a text chat conversation going on in tandem with the focal oral instructional conversation. They can thereby make jokes, ask each other and instructors questions, etc.

Providing implicit feedback

As we have just seen, there are numerous techniques common to language classrooms whereby instructors explicitly comment on and correct what learners say and write. Indeed, providing explicit feedback is a mainstay of a good deal of learning in general. Language education, however, is unique in this respect because while learners are attending to what they say and write in the target language, they are at the same time learning the language they are producing while communicating meaningful things. This, as many researchers have pointed out, is cognitively and affectively demanding work. To interrupt learners as they undertake this complex process of production and comprehension, whether it is to insert a comment or to overtly correct their grammar, pronunciation or word choice is to potentially derail their utterance in the making. The alternative to explicit feedback and the risk of pushing learners off track is the use of implicit feedback such as recasts, echoing, in tandem with the visual and aural cueing attendant to synchronous oral online environments.

Recasts

A recast is 'a well-formed reformulation of a learner's non-target utterance with the original meaning intact' (Lyster, 2004: 403). It is feeding back to the learner his or her utterance with any errors in form, word choice or pronunciation/intonation corrected and orally and/or in text emphasizing the corrected portion. Recasts are ideally spoken in such a way as to be conversational and thereby not disruptive of the ongoing exchange. While recasts appear to be an effective strategy to preserve the flow of conversation while drawing attention to students' errors, in live classrooms they carry the risk of passing by unnoticed by learners. Synchronous oral online venues, however, have tools and features that support teacher and student recasts while (1) the meaning-making aspect of the conversation is sustained; (2) attention is visually drawn to the correct, recasted form; and (3) an archive of the recasted portions of conversations can be utilized to further draw attention to and review the focal language as it was used.

In an advanced intermediate EFL course, a learner misuses the focal form (might have been) for the task of speculating on the motives for a crime. The *might have been* form is in the **task toolkit** and both instructor and students are monitoring the utterances produced for the correct construction of this form during the task. When a student makes an error in producing the correct form, fellow students type the correct form into the text box and/or point to the correct form in the **task toolkit** as a form of recast. If this is insufficient, the instructor or another student can speak (recast) the correct form while visual attention is drawn to the text representations.

S1:   He might have stole that painting.
S2:   Stolen (*circles the word "stolen"; Figure 26*)

Figure 26 Recasts in oral synchronous environments

Recasting as a non-intrusive instructional conversation strategy often takes place in an online class in the same way it does in an f2f classroom as in this example from an online Russian lesson.

S1:   Весной я люблю работать в саде. [In spring I like to work in the garden (*erroneous ending*)]

S2:   Ты бегаешь летом на улице? [Do you run along the street?]

S1:   Нет. Никогда не бегаю. [No, I never run.]

S3:   Ты сказала, ты работаешь в саде? [You said you worked in the garden (*erroneous ending*)]

T: В саду. [In the garden (*corrected ending*)]

S3:   В саду. [In the garden (*correct ending*)]

S1:   I must've said it wrong. В саду. [In the garden (*correct ending*)]

Sometimes, however, recasting can be visual. Instructors either replace or supply oral recasting with visual ones.

S: Ты давно ждает Ивана? [For how long do you wait (*incorrect form*) for Ivan?]

T: Ты давно..? [For how long do you ...?] (*switches to one of the previous slides and circles the correct form for the verb "to wait" in the conjugation table as shown in Figure 27*)

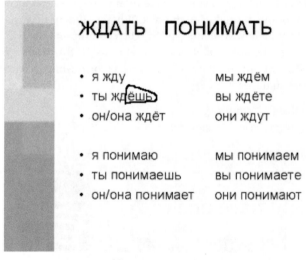

Figure 27 Visual recast

S: Ты давно ждёшь... ждёшь Ивана? [For how long do you wait (*correct ending*)... do you wait (*correct ending*) for Ivan?]

Meaning/Form-focused feedback

Meaning/Form-focused feedback is different from recasting in that it is part of a natural continuation of a conversation with the corrected student's utterances integrated into the communicative stream without making it obvious. It is 'provided as a part of an authentic conversation on the topic of the learner's personal interest without discourse derailment'

(Meskill & Anthony, 2005: 100). Seedhouse (1997) called such corrective feedback 'camouflaged' repair. The difference between recast and meaning/form feedback is that recasts are exact repetitions of students' utterances with only one form corrected. On the contrary, meaning/form-focused feedback consists of a teacher's response to the student's utterance, with only one piece of the student's utterance corrected and injected into the teacher's utterance with the teacher's utterance being a natural part of the conversation. Meaning/form-focused feedback is often followed by linguistic traps, or questions forcing learners to answer, using vocabulary or grammatical structures that appear to be problematic to them. Table 1 provides an example of how the same initial erroneous statement can be treated in recast, corrective recast, meaning/form-focused feedback and modeling.

Table 1 Examples of the differences between recasts, corrective recasts, meaning/form-focused feedback and models

Recast	Corrective recast	Meaning/Form-focused feedback	Models
The corrected problematic form is used as a part of the initial utterance.	The corrected problematic form is used as a part of the initial utterance supplied with linguistic and nonlinguistic cues.	The corrected problematic form is used as a part of a natural conversation.	The corrected problematic form is used several times in different contexts.
S: I drinked tea yesterday. T: I drank tea yesterday.	S: I drinked tea yesterday. T: I DRANK (stressed) tea yesterday.	S: I drinked tea yesterday. T: I drank coffee. I don't like tea at all. Did you drink coffee, too?	S: I drinked tea yesterday. T: Drank. I drank coffee. He drank milk. She drank juice.

The effectiveness of meaning/form-focused feedback as compared to, for instance, corrective recasts, can be questionable. While this instructional move proved to be working in written asynchronous environments as a non-disruptive part of authentic conversations in text-based discussion forums (Meskill & Anthony, 2005), its impact on language acquisition in the oral mode with its lack of visualization and time affordances can be undermined by the specifics of the medium. There is some evidence, however, that equipped with visual and voice characteristics, meaning/form-focused feedback can be noticed by the students and, hence, be instructionally effective.

In a warm-up activity, a Russian instructor asks a student whether she has a car. The student confirms, mispronouncing the word 'car' in her answer. The instructor keeps asking details about the student's car, modeling the correct use of the word for the student and forcing her to follow the model.

T: У тебя есть машина? (Do you have a car?)
S: Да, у меня есть масина. [Yes, I do have a car (*pronunciation error*).]
T: Тебе нравится твоя машина? [Do you like your car?] (*deliberately distinguish pronunciation of the word "car"*)

S: О да! [Oh yes!] (*laughing*) It's Mitsubishi Gallant. Очень очень хорошая. [Very very nice.]

T: Какого цвета твоя машина? Синяя? [What color is your car? Blue?] (*quickly draws a car with a digital blue marker and writes "машина" [car]*)

S: Моя машина красная. [My car (*correct pronunciation*) is red.]

T: Твоя машина новая или старая? [Is your car new or old?]

S: Моя машина новая [My car is new (*correct pronunciation*)].

Thus, the meaning/form-focused feedback in the form of implicit correction gets integrated into the meaningful conversation. When supplied with intonation and text clues, this is a central working model for oral synchronous online environments.

Echoing

Synchronous oral environments lend themselves particularly well to oral/written echoing of learner output. Echoing is repeating back what the student has said as a method of drawing attention to errors while requesting a reformulation. Synchronous oral environments work well as instructors can signal their request for reformulation via the intonation of their voice. Simultaneously, they can signal where in the utterance the error has occurred in visual (text with highlighting) ways. These multimodal echoes ensure that learners attend to both the fact that a reformulation is requested and to what in the utterance needs to be amended.

In the following example, a beginning level EFL learner has been describing his trip to the doctor's office. The focal form in this task's **task toolkit** is the irregular past tense.

S: Then I tell her, the doctor, I tell

T: I *tell* her?

As she echoes, the instructor also points to the list of irregular past verb forms in the **task toolkit**. Attention to voice and/or visual can thereby assist the speaker in modifying his output using the correct form of the verb.

Summary

The affordances of synchronous oral online environments allow for the extension and amplification of the kinds of instructional conversations language educators typically conduct in live classrooms. By considering these multimodal tools and resources as means for such support, language educators can maximize the teaching and learning possibilities they represent. We have examined our eight instructional conversation strategies and sample ways in which they can be undertaken using the tools and resources of the environment to best effect. We will approach the other three online learning environments similarly in the following chapters.

References

Levy, M. and Kennedy, C. (2004) A task-cycling pedagogy using audio-conferencing as stimulated reflection for foreign language learning. *Language Learning & Technology* 8 (2), 50–68.

Lyster, R. (2004) Differential effects of prompts and recasts in form-focused instruction. *Studies in Second Language Acquisition* 26, 399–432.

Meskill, C. and Anthony, N. (2005) Foreign language learning with CMC: Forms of instructional discourse in a hybrid Russian class. *System* 33 (1), 89–105.

Meskill, C. and Anthony, N. (2007) Form-focused communicative practice via computer mediated communication: What language learners say. *Computer Assisted Language Instruction Consortium Journal* 25 (1), 69–90.

Seedhouse, P. (1997) Combining meaning and form. *English Language Teaching Journal* 51, 336–344.

Wang, Y. (2004) Distance language learning: Interactivity and fourth-generation Internet-based videoconferencing. *The Computer Assisted Language Instruction Consortium Journal* 21 (2), 373–395.

Wang, Y. (2006) Negotiation of meaning in desktop videoconferencing-supported distance language learning. *ReCALL* 18 (1), 122–145.

End of chapter notes

Instructional conversations in *informal* oral synchronous online environments

The preceding examples of instructional conversations in oral synchronous environments are based on formal, instructor-led conversations. It is important to note that these instructional conversation strategies work equally well in less formal oral synchronous environments. As language learners seek opportunities to practice and receive additive feedback informally on the internet (PalTalk, iVisit, NetMeeting, Skype, Yahoo Voice Chat, AOL Voice Chat, Windows Messenger, etc.), casual online conversation partners can find themselves being asked to instruct. A common plea of 'please correct my English/Japanese/Russian' can be met by observing here how instructional conversations support language learning and apply these in informal environments.

Translation

When is translation a good option? At lower proficiency levels, translation (using the instructor and learners' common non-target language) is a very useful tool for dealing with course management. In this context it serves as an expedient and might thereby be best considered an expedient throughout instruction with the proviso that translating may represent a missed learning opportunity, a missed teachable moment. It is up to the instructor to continually weigh these two considerations. In synchronous environments where time is a premium commodity, expedience may outweigh all else. As we will see in asynchronous environments, expedience is eliminated and translation, therefore, becomes less useful.

Moreover, in online environments translation can be significantly reduced and even eliminated due to instantaneous access to digital resources based on the needs of learners and instructors. In oral synchronous environments there are ample opportunities for avoiding excessive use of the target language in task explanations, for example, a Russian instructor directs the task almost entirely in the target language with the help of different visuals to which she refers (Figure 28).

T: Let's imagine you're visiting one of your friends. Вы пришли в гости к другу. И вы звоните в дверь. [You came to visit your friend. And you ring the door bell.] (*circling several times the picture with the thumb on the doorbell*). Но вы не знаете, здесь ваш друг живёт или нет. [But you don't know whether your friend lives here or not.] (*drawing a question mark on the picture with the woman ringing the doorbell*) Какой-то человек открывает дверь. И вы спрашиваете: «Здесь живёт Валентина Ивановна Петрова?» [Some person opens the door. And you ask "Does Valentina Ivanovna Petrova live here?" (*circling the bullet next to the first line that asks this question*). И вам говорят: «Да, здесь.» [And you are answered: "Yes, here." (*circling the next bullet with these words*) А вы говорите: Она дома? [And you say: "Is she at home?] (*circling the next bullet*) И вам говорят: «Да, дома.» [And you are told "Yes, at home." (*circling the next bullet*) (*short pause*) Вместо имени «Валентина Петровна Петрова» [Instead of the name of Valentina Ivanovna Petrova...] (*crossing out the name*) говорите другие имена из этого списка, например, Татьяна Владимировна Майорова. [...say different names from this list, for example, Tatyana Vladimirovna Mayorova.] (*underscoring the name from the list and drawing an arrow from the name used in the model to one of the names in the list*)

Figure 28 Avoiding translation

In this example, combining images and connecting them with non-verbal clues such as circling, underscoring, crossing out and drawing arrows can substitute for a translation.

In oral synchronous environments, translation can also be undertaken with the use of visuals. The instructor uses arrows to point out the Russian equivalent of an English word. The instructor wants to make sure that the students understand the difference between two constructions: 'It's ... o'clock' and 'At ... o'clock'. The difference between them is in adding the preposition B [at] to the latter.

T: "At" по-русски будет "в." ["At" in Russian will be "V".] (*draws an arrow from the English preposition to its Russian equivalent; Figure 29*)

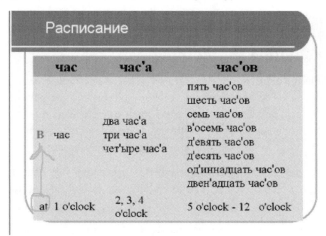

Figure 29 Supplementing translations

End of chapter activities

Activity A. Oral synchronous environment affordances

For each of the eight instructional conversation strategies discussed for oral synchronous online environments, how can each of the following affordances be capitalized on for language teaching and learning?

Affordances	1	2	3	4	5	6	7	8
Convenience								
Connectivity								
Membership (playfield is leveled)								
Authentic audiences								
Tailored audiences								
Strategies to compensate for lack of non-verbal info								
Richness of information (links, multimedia)								
Time to focus and review								
Time to compose, resources to compose								
Time and opportunity to reflect								
Opportunity to witness and track learning								
Opportunity to demonstrate learning								

Key to table: 1. Calling attention to forms; 2. Calling attention to lexis; 3. Corralling; 4. Saturating; 5. Using linguistic traps; 6. Modeling; 7. Providing explicit feedback; 8. Providing implicit feedback

Activity B. Online literacy skills

Review the online literacy skills that digital natives possess (Chapter 1, pp. 13–14). For each of the examples of instructional conversation in this chapter, discuss if and how these skills are employed. If they are not, could they be? What are the advantages of exploiting these skills for language learning purposes?

Activity C. Evaluating the learning

A rubric is an excellent teaching and learning tool. It helps in course design and when making adjustments based on student learning. For students, it assists them in realizing what is expected of them, how far they have developed, and the learning that remains to be done. In oral synchronous environments, rubrics can be one of many windowed resources which all can consult prior to, during and after a synchronous session.

Select one of the language learning tasks described in this chapter. For this task, develop an evaluation rubric with which both teacher and student can assess the language learning that took place.

Create a matrix that contains the four portions of an evaluation rubric:

- description of the task;

- levels of performance while undertaking the task;

- the evaluation dimensions: comprehension, pronunciation, syntax, lexis (you decide);

- description exemplary performance for dimensions (Scoring guide).

Rubric

Task description:

Dimensions	Competent	Developing	Needs work

Scoring guide

Task description:

Dimensions	Description of competent performance	Comments

Once you and your students are accustomed to using rubrics productively, students can be asked to develop these on their own, complete them and submit them as part of an individual electronic portfolio that reflects their learning of the language. This kind of self-assessment can be highly motivating, especially for students who are learning 100% online.

Activity D. Applying instructional strategies to the task

Analyze the following example from an oral synchronous lesson and identify the instructional strategies it contains. The task is for students working in pairs to survey each other about the places they have visited using pictures provided of famous places. The **task toolkit** at the top of the slide provides an example of a question to be asked (Figure 30).

Figure 30 Simulated oral synchronous lesson

S1:   Have you ever been in Japanese?

S2:   In Japan? No, I have never been in Japan. Have you ever been in... What is that on that picture? At the bottom?

S1:   I'm not sure. Dessert?

T: Actually, it's not a desert even though it looks like a desert. It's the Great Wall of China.

S1:   Oh I see. Have you ever been in China?

S2:   No, I have never been in China. Have you ever... Is it a Croatian church?

T: (switches on the application sharing feature and shows several pictures of Russia stored on her desktop)

S2:   So it's Russia then. Have you ever in Russia?

T: (*circles the word "been" that was missed by the student*)

S2:   (*laughing*) Have you ever been in Russia?

S1:   Yes. I have been in Russia. Actually I live in Russia till I was 10.

S2:   You lived in Russia? So you are Russian, right?

Activity E. Designing and conducting a task for the oral synchronous environment

Design a five-minute mini-task to be used in an oral synchronous environment. Conduct your task with your classmates functioning as your students via any available oral synchronous venue. You can use such free applications as Skype or Yahoo Voice Chat. Use as many of the eight instructional conversation strategies as possible. Make notes while observing other classmates' mini-tasks.

Activity F. Analyzing instructional conversation strategies

Discuss your own and your classmates' mini-tasks. What instructional conversation strategies were used? What instructional conversation strategies appeared to be the most/least effective from your point of view? What factors have contributed to the degree of effectiveness of these instructional conversation strategies? Complete the matrix below.

Instructional strategies	Most effective	Least effective	Factors influenced
1			
2			
3			
4			
5			
6			
7			
8			

Activity G. Creating a lesson plan

Create a lesson plan for a 30-minute oral synchronous online lesson for the language you teach. Include tasks and activities that you see as suitable for this environment. Provide a rationale for your design.

Activity H. Analyzing lesson plans

Analyze your own lesson plan. How does the knowledge of the eight instructional conversation strategies you have learned about in this chapter and the affordances/limitations of the oral synchronous environment influence your way of organizing the materials, tasks and activities? Write a one-page reflection, answering these questions.

Further reading

Arcos de los, B. and Arnedillo Sánchez, I. (2006) Ears before Eyes: Expanding tutors' interaction skills beyond physical presence in audio-graphic collaborative virtual learning environments. In P. Zaphiris and G. Zacharia (eds) *User-Centered Computer Aided Language Learning* (pp. 74–93). Hershey: Idea Group, Inc.

Cziko, G. and Park, S. (2003) Internet audio communication for second language learning: A comparative review of six programs. *Language Learning & Technology* 7 (1), 15–27.

Hampel, R. and Hauck, M. (2004) Towards an effective use of audio conferencing in distance language courses. *Language Learning & Technology* 8 (1), 66–82.

Kötter, M. (2001) Developing distance language learners' interactive competence – can synchronous audio do the trick? *International Journal of Educational Telecommunications* 7 (4), 327–353.

Rosell-Aguilar, F. (2005) Task design for audiographic conferencing: Promoting beginner oral interaction in distance language learning. *Computer Assisted Language Learning* 18 (5), 417–442.

3

Language learning and teaching in oral asynchronous online environments

- Oral asynchronous environments, their special affordances for language education, are discussed.

- Descriptions and representations of how instructional conversations are carried out in these environments are presented.

- Limitations for practical use of the oral asynchronous mode are outlined.

Language learning and teaching in oral asynchronous online environments

Objectives

In this chapter you will learn:

- the definition of oral asynchronous online environments;

- the special affordances of oral asynchronous online environments;

- how different instructional conversation strategies can be undertaken in these environments;

- how the environment's affordances can be taken advantage of to support and amplify these conversations;

- methods of formative evaluation of student learning in oral asynchronous modes.

Oral asynchronous online environments are venues where individuals and groups can post recorded audio messages. Accompanying these audio messages can be visual and textual information. Venues for posting and sharing these multimodal messages can be almost any telecommunications medium: email, blogs, message boards, community messaging sites, etc. For individuals wishing to learn and practice another language, there are a number of publically accessible oral asynchronous sites whereby they can seek out tutors and conversation partners with whom to exchange such multimodal messages (see list of Free resources, p. 190).

The chief difference between the online environment described in the previous chapter (oral synchronous) and the online environment described in this chapter (oral asynchronous) is, of course, the issue of synchronicity. We will see the same central contrast between Chapters 5 and 6, written synchronous and written asynchronous. The difference between real time versus delayed time in online communication is vast in terms of the essential nature of the communication process. When it comes to teaching and learning in general, this difference becomes substantial; the time one has to think, assimilate and compose making a world of difference. When it comes to teaching and learning *language*, this difference is tremendous, most notably as regards affect; time being a second language learner's largest hurdle for comprehending and producing meaningful target language utterances.

With oral asynchronous modes, language learners have the luxury of time to repeat recorded messages, access resources, and thereby comprehend and strategize their responses. In composing their responses, they can again enjoy the luxury of unlimited time with which to rehearse, record and revise their posts. Likewise, instructors can take their time to develop and construct their instructional conversation strategies in response to learners. The affordance of being able to scan, recap and repeat an audio post as many times as needed can be capitalized on to focus on both comprehending native speaker recordings and in attending to and practicing the phonological features of the target language. Moreover, instructors and learners can use their voice in conjunction with other modalities to draw attention to certain linguistic features and to optimize the intonation features that shape conversations. As we will see in this chapter, the asynchronous aspect, along with the oral/aural, hold numerous possibilities in this regard.

Note: Unlike the oral synchronous online environment, an entire language course, indeed a good portion of a language course, would be cumbersome in the oral asynchronous mode only. In combination with the other three modes, however, it is a viable supplement especially when the emphasis is on listening and speaking development in the target language. Additionally, the oral asynchronous mode works nicely as a complement to blended courses: courses which take place partly face-to-face, and partly online.

Voice worksheets
Voice journals
Voice emails
Voice boards
Voice post-its
Voice over presentations
Voice over tours of work accomplished

Calling attention to forms

In generating multimodal posts for language learners, instructors can consider the numerous combinatorial possibilities to draw learner attention to forms under study or that appear in student posts and are in need of attention/repair. Using voice plus image, plus text in any combination can guide learners to attend to highlighted aspects of the spoken and or written language. Again, the advantage of asynchronous multimodal messages is the comprehending, planning and composing time afforded to both learners and instructors in employing these kinds of attention-drawing strategies.

If, for example, a learner submits an audio file of their response to an instructor's question, instructor oral responses can be inserted and embedded into the student's original file for review. In the following example an EFL learner submitted a brief monolog in response to the instructor's prompt, 'Tell us about your weekend'. On reviewing the learner's submission, the instructor locates mistakes in the use of the simple past tense, the focus of current coursework. Using a simple audio editing program, she interleaves her prompts which call attention to the focal forms that the learner has misused:

S: And I have a good time at party...
T: You "have" a good time?

In response to the instructor's prompt the student then re-records his original monolog making the corrections as the teacher has indicated.

Recording tasks such as this simple one can be powerful forms of close study and review of learner performance. Inserting prompts and corrections after the fact is an ideal approach to encouraging fluency (while speaking) while coaching attention to focal forms.

Task-level attention to form

As in the above brief example, task-level attention to form can be nicely achieved using oral asynchronous modes. Moreover, in this mode, learners have as many opportunities as they need to refer to the focal task information in the **task toolkit** as they record, review and re-record their posts. This form of self-assessment and self-monitoring can help build and hone these very useful language learning strategies for future implementation throughout the language learning enterprise. This is a particularly attractive aspect of the oral asynchronous mode.

This example from an online Russian course demonstrates the use of a voice board for a role play activity, 'The new recreation room.' Students are asked to virtually furnish their new recreation room on campus, using the vocabulary and grammatical structures that are the focus of the lesson: furniture, spatial prepositions and verbs of placement. While in English, there is only one verb 'to put' used for placing objects to hang in horizontal, or vertical positions, Russian has three verbs for indicating these actions. The task is: 'For this week, you will have a Voice Discussion that will be conducted through the Wimba Voice Board. The topic of this voice discussion is "The New Recreation Room". Imagine that there is a new recreation room for online Russian students on campus. You have a limited budget to buy furniture and other stuff and then furnish and decorate this room. Submit at least three messages discussing your decoration plans'. Model: - Давайте поставим диван к стене. – Хорошо. Давайте повесим русский флаг над диваном. – Нет, давайте лучше повесим русский ковёр над диваном [- Let's put the sofa next to the wall. – OK. Let's hang a Russian flag above the sofa. – No, let's put a Russian rug above the sofa.] (Figure 31). The information in the task toolkit is in both written and in oral forms. Students listen to the models by clicking on the play button. Students are also provided with references to the meaning with the visuals indicating the differences in actions and examples containing grammatical peculiarities in form changes (Figure 32).

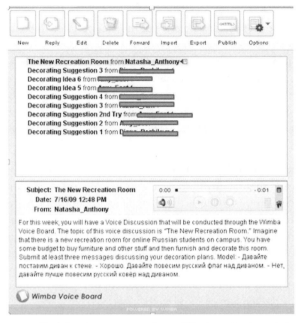

Figure 31 Task-level attention to form. Wimba voice board thread

Verbs of Placement II

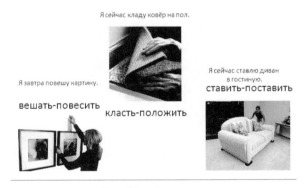

Figure 32 Task toolkit. The new recreation room

Student 1: Давайте поставим диван у стены. Давайте поставим торшер справа от дивана. [Let's put a sofa next to the wall. Let's put the floor lamp to the right from the sofa.]

Student 2: Давайте поставим диван в центре комнаты и повесим домашний кинотеатр на стену. Давайте поставим бильярд за диваном. [Let's put the sofa in the middle of the room and put the home theater on the wall. Let's put the billiard table behind the sofa.]

Student 3: Я тоже хочу бильярд. Но я думаю, бильярд надо поставить в центр комнаты. [I want the billiard, too. But I think we should put the billiard in the middle of the room.]

Student 1: Хорошо. Давайте поставим бильярд в центре комнаты, но давайте поставим диван возле стены. [Good. Let's put the billiard table in the middle of the room but let's put the sofa next to the wall.]

Student 2: Ладно, ребята. Давайте поставим бильярд в центре комнаты и поставим диван у стены. Что вы думаете о домашнем кинотеатре? Вы хотите это или нет? [OK guys. Let's put the billiard in the middle of the room and sofa next to the wall. What do you think about a home theater? Do you want one or not?]

Student 3: Согласна. Но надо повесить телевизор на стену напротив дивана. [Agreed. But we have to put a TV on the wall across from the sofa.]

This example shows that the oral nature of this activity is instrumental in developing students' oral skills and their ability to freely communicate in Russian in an attempt to reach a reasonable compromise. The asynchronous nature of this activity helps the students concentrate on the formal aspects of their utterances by checking dictionaries and grammar notes. They also had time to think and plan before recording these messages. The oral asynchronous mode provides an opportunity then for students to use Russian at a higher level of proficiency while decreasing beginners' language anxiety. Students can play back their classmates' messages as many times as they want or need to, which helps them develop listening comprehension skills as well.

In the following example, beginning learners of ESL/EFL are assigned a role play activity whereby pairs are asked to practice, then record and post a conversation (Figures 33 and 34). The scene is in a restaurant with one learner playing the role of the waiter and the other the customer. In the **task toolkit** are the following structures and lexis:

Waiter:
Can I take your order?
That's a (repeat back customer's order)
Anything else?
Thank you.

Customer:
I would like....
And can I please have...
That's all.
Thank you.

A menu in simplified English is provided for the pair to use in developing their recording. Once the pair has rehearsed and recorded this assignment (note: if learners are geographically distant, this can be accomplished via oral synchronous means), they post the draft audio assignment to either a course site or the particular public forum that the class uses for such purposes. Both the instructor and classmates can then review the pairwork, insert audio comments and corrections to the pair's uses of the target forms, and/or leave written comments and questions for the pair to address.

An intermediate learner of ESL/EFL submits the following post in response to the Voice Board assignment 'Who is your favorite movie star? Imagine you meet this person in real life. Invite them to have coffee with you'.

Figure 33 Task-level attention to form

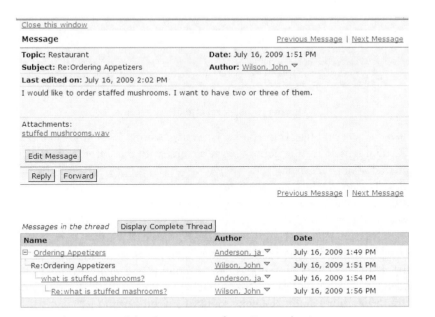

Figure 34 Task-level attention to form. Text and voice message

The **task toolkit** contains the following in both text and audio with intonation of humble requests an integral part of the focal language (Figure 35):

> Would you possible consider...
> Do you think you might do me the honor of...
> Would you maybe have the time to...

Figure 35 Task-level attention to form

S1:   (*written and spoken*) I like Tom Hanks. He is my favorite. I would say to him: Do you think you might do me the honor to have a coffee with me? [pronunciation of think, might and honor very weak]

S2:   (*written*) Try, do me the *honor of having*

S1:   (*written*) OK. Listen to me now. (*spoken*) Do you think you might do me the honor of having a coffee with me?

T: (*written*) Nice job, Naomi. Now, listen to me. Pay special attention to my pronunciation of the ends of words. (*written with consonants in caps and spoken*) Do you thinK you mighT do me the honor of having coffee with me? (*rising invitation intonation*).

S1:   (*written*) OK. I try again. Listen. (*spoken*) Hello, Mr. Hanks. I like you very much. Do you think you might do me the honor of having a coffee with me?

S3:   (*written*) Is it coffee or *a* coffee?

S2:   (*written*) I think *a* coffee, no?

T: (*written*) Coffee is most often a non-count noun but informally people use it as a count noun, *a* coffee meaning "a cup of coffee". Now listen to my pronunciation. (*spoken*). Do you think you might do me the honor of having coffee with me?

Incidental attention to forms

There are several ways that oral asynchronous messages can be used incidentally throughout online learning processes in order to draw learners' attention to forms. In the process of responding to learners' posts, instructors and other students can use a combination of text and recorded audio to simultaneously address the meaning of the learner's post and to visually, aurally and textually draw their attention to any mistakes or gaps in the language they used in constructing it. Indeed, responses can be specifically labeled as addressing meaning or pronunciation or intonation, etc.

During an open asynchronous discussion about a current event, an advanced ESL/EFL learner makes a mistake using the English gerund. Doing a quick search of her pre-recorded library of audio reminder files, the instructor locates the appropriate file and adds it as an audio post-it note to the student's post.

S: I enjoyed to cook dinner last night.
T: (*audio file attached*) Remember, we use the –ing form with the verb *enjoy*. For example, I enjoy going to the theater.

Incidental attention to form can take place in a structured activity focused on specific forms. This example demonstrates how a Russian instructor structures a discussion activity on students' likes, dislikes and favorites by asking them questions. The focal form is the use of possessive pronouns in their masculine, feminine and neuter forms (Figure 36). The instructor notices that one of the students uses the word 'музыканта' (an incorrect feminine form of the noun 'музыкант' [musician]). She seized the opportunity to remind this student that the noun 'музыкант' [musician] has only a masculine form by asking her questions requiring the use of this word in this specific context.

Figure 36 Incidental attention to form

S: Моя любимая музыканта – Кортни Лав. [My favorite musician (*incorrect form*) – Courtny Love.

T: А мой любимый музыкант – Вики Мартинез. А любимый музыкант Жаклин – Ля Тойя Джексон. [And my favorite musician (*correct form*) is Vicci Martinez. And Jacqueline's favorite musician is La Toya Jackson.]

Incidental attention to form can certainly take place in informal, non-instructional asynchronous audio conferencing between NS–NNS or NS–NS. Voxopop is one of the sites that allows for free and open oral asynchronous interactions among native and non-native speakers of world languages (Figure 37).

Figure 37 Incidental attention to form

In the forum 'What is your favorite car and why?' the following incidental focus on form takes place regarding the word 'inexpensive'.

NNS1:   My favorite car is Nissan Rouge. It's reliable, fast, and inexpensive /.../.

NNS2:   My favorite car is Mazda-6. It is so fast. They call it zoom-zoom how fast it is. /.../ But I cannot say it's unexpensive... inexpensive?.. inexpensive (laughing).

NNS3:   /.../ There are not too many inexpensive cars that are nice.

Calling attention to lexis

Oral asynchronous modes are particularly useful for learning and reinforcing new vocabulary in the target language. Like in the oral synchronous examples we examined in Chapter 2, there are ample opportunities for teachers and learners to access visual equivalents and translations for new words and expressions in online venues. Oral recording can be made use of to model the pronunciation of new words and to model their use in spoken contexts. Indeed, by making and collecting audio clips of many different native speakers using the target words or phrases, learners can hear new words spoken by those with a range of dialects and speaking patterns, thus extending their ability to comprehend in contexts and situations well beyond the language instruction environment.

Task-level attention to lexis

The design of any solid language learning task requires that focal vocabulary needed for successful task processes be reviewed and highlighted in some manner. This can be accomplished in any number of ways using the oral asynchronous in conjunction with other modalities: text, visuals, video, animations, etc. These multimodalities can both enliven the **task toolkit** where focal vocabulary can be continually accessed and attention drawn, as well as inserted in ongoing task conversations for clarification and calling attention to features such as pronunciation and appropriate use.

Again, the greatest affordance of oral asynchronous modes is the control learners can exercise over how much and how often a recorded sequence is repeated and the capacity to rerecord posts until a communicative standard is met. That also means that any online resources that might aid comprehension and production can be accessed at the same time. Such resources to support understanding and using new vocabulary come in the form of (1) intonation within audio posts that highlight a word use and its meaning; (2) visual supports to link meaning; (3) and highlighting text that support meaning.

In an intermediate ESL/EFL discussion on talking about the weather, the instructor uses intonation in her oral asynchronous post to draw learners' attention to a new lexical item.

T: It's too *chilly* (brrr sound) to go swimming.

This audio post is inserted in a student post about the weather and outdoor activities in order to draw attention to a potentially novel lexical item that can be used in subsequent discussion.

In the same intermediate ESL/EFL discussion, the instructor pastes in a video clip of a dark, lightening-filled sky accompanied by the sounds of thunder along with her audio post (Figure 38):

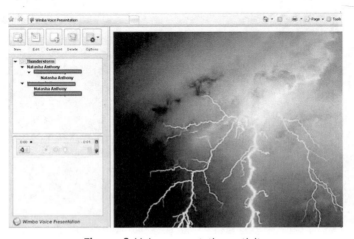

Figure 38 Voice presentation activity.

T: We need to be careful during thunderstorms.

Finally, in the same discussion, the instructor simply uses visual highlighting of a focal lexical item, highlighting that indicates that by clicking on the highlighted word, an audio version of the word will play (Figure 39).

T: We'll need to keep an eye on the barometer.

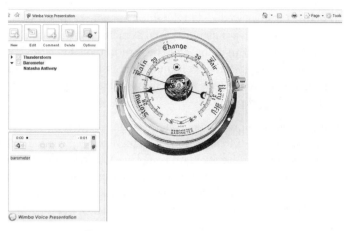

Figure 39 Voice presentation activity

To call attention to lexis, instructors use both visual and voice emphases. An ESL instructor provides students with instances of common phrases used to talk about the weather. While she reads these phrases, she underscores them on the slide (Figure 40).

T: SUNNY (*underscores the word*). IT'S SUNNY (*underscores the phrase*)

Figure 40 Visuals and voice

In this next example the focus is on teaching Turkish words denoting food for beginners. It is called 'A Tour of a Turkish Breakfast'. The teacher makes pictures of food which she supplies with English transliterations (Figure 41).

T: (*written*) Here we have a selection of Turkish breads. They're all salty. The round rings are covered in sesame seeds. They're sold on the street all day long and make a simple, cheap snack. (*oral*) They are called "simit" and white bread is called "ekmek." Hmm... (*laughing*) actually my last name is Smith and as Turkish doesn't have a "th" sound and doesn't allow consonant clusters at the beginning of the words, people can't say Smith and they end up saying "simit." Simit. Simit. Which makes me sound like a bread roll (*laughing*)

Figure 41 Visuals, text and voice

Incidental attention to lexis

As we discussed in the context of the oral synchronous mode, visuals can be called up at any time during online conversations to clarify the meaning of unfamiliar lexical items. The oral asynchronous mode is distinct in that both instructors and students have the luxury of more time to assemble and post multimodal messages. For incidentally occurring vocabulary words with which learners struggle, they can, for example, be asked to repeat the word five or ten times, use it in a sentence, then use it in a question. This recorded post can be saved in a learner's personal online space for review at any time, prior to a quiz, for example.

In voice discussions, voice messages are often accompanied by text remarks, usually functioning as organizing or clarifying tools when incidental focus on lexis occurs. A group of English learners discusses the topic 'Have you ever been influenced by a movie?' While the oral conversation between two interlocutors is entirely on the topic whereby they provide their own examples of the movies and reasons why they influenced them, their text messages are focused on clarifying the title of the movie (Figure 42).

Figure 42 Voice and text

NNS1:   (*oral*) /.../ I watched several musical films like *Phantom of the Opera* and /.../. It is so impressive /.../. I haven't watched the *Chicago* yet. And you mentioned about the film about the Jewish family. I want to know the title. Please type the title of the film you've mentioned in the message option. (*written*) Please type the title of the film about the jewish family.

NNS2:   (*oral*) /.../ I don't have any program telling you the title of the movie especially I think that you should see it. It's amazing. For the topic, for the actors and also for the music. The music is it is classical but it is also musical. It is amazing. It's just amazing. /.../ (*written*) the title is "the fiddler of the roof."

In the following example, participants focus on lexical items with the help of both voice and text. A group of English learners practice their English skills by playing a question and answer game. Each participant is to answer a question in the previous voice message and ask his own question for the next person.

NNS1:   (*oral*) It's the middle of the summer. It is so hot. My question is what flavor of the ice cream do you like?

NNS2:   (*written*) coffee + rum raisin (Figure 43) (*oral*) When I want an ice cream, I always ask for two flavors, and this two flavors are coffee and rum raisin.

Figure 43 Incidental attention to lexis

Corralling

Task-level corralling

One of the most effective methods of corralling learners into using a focal form or lexical item is using an audio dubbing assignment. This kind of activity makes excellent use of the oral asynchronous mode. Learners are assigned a brief video clip with no audio. The video can depict either people talking, in which case a learner or learners would be charged with dubbing their voices, or a documentary-like scene in which case a learner or learners would be assigned to provide commentary for the visuals (Figure 44). The visual context and content of the video clips can be aligned with current focal target language and/or language for review. Appropriate **task toolkits** can thereby be made accessible for learners to access while undertaking the assignment. The dubbed audio portions can then be reviewed and evaluated by both instructor and peers.

Figure 44 Task-level corralling. Dubbing

(*the video displays two women talking*)

S1: Здравствуйте, Татьяна Денисовна. Как у вас дела? [Hello, Tatiana Denisovna. How are you doing?]

S2: Хорошо, Лена. А у тебя? [Good, Lena. How are you?]

S1: Неплохо. [Not bad.]

The **task toolkit** with the greeting/farewell phrases is provided to students in both written and oral forms.

Another means of task-level corralling in the oral asynchronous mode consists of posting recorded instructor utterances that steer the requisite response to use the focal forms and/or lexis for the task at hand. In the next scenario, a pair of beginning ESL/EFL learners has posted their audio post assignment of a direction asking and giving role play task. The focal forms in the task's **task toolkit** consist of the following vocabulary items:

across from
next to
right
left
corner
on the ___

turn
walk
you will see

The **task toolkit** contains picture icons of those items as in Figure 45.

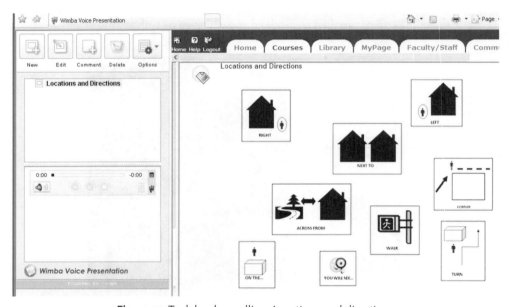

Figure 45 Task-level corralling. Locations and directions

A simple map of labeled city streets and landmarks is provided along with the model dialog (Figure 46).

On review of the one pair's recorded role play, the instructor notes that both learners are inserting an extra 'to' in their sentences; e.g. You turn to right, You turn to left. In her recorded post, she says the following to the pair.

T: I see. You turn RIGHT at CHURCH Street, then you turn LEFT at STATE Street. Can you please repeat these directions. WHERE do you turn?

She thereby corrals the learner into supplying the appropriate form. The beauty of the oral synchronous mode is that learners can replay this post as many times as they need to hear the correct form and the instructor can repost the post as many times as need be for the learners to attend to the correct model. At any time, the instructor can also complement her post with visuals representing the oral directions.

Figure 46 Task-level corralling. Locations and directions

An ESL teacher provides mid-beginning students with a picture asking them to discuss what they think is going on in the picture. Students discuss possible choices. They are reminded via a **task toolkit** that they are expected to use vocabulary to express emotions in ways that involve participles such as 'scared', 'thrilled', 'surprised', 'stressed', etc. (Figure 47).

T: Tell the story about this picture using your own voice.

Figure 47 Task-level corralling. Emotions

As an extension, the instructor can ask students to upload pictures on a given topic and describe them using an appropriate **toolkit** in the archives. In the following example, ESL students are asked to find funny sport pictures and describe them in English.

S: (*uploads the picture as in Figure 48*) (*oral*) This player is caught and stuck on the net. He run over speed limit and lost his control. So nobody in the team could unlock him.

Figure 48 Corralling

In being asked to describe events in a picture, students are corralled into using, in this case, constructions with past tense action verbs 'ran', 'got', 'hit', 'laughed', etc.

Incidental corralling

At any point in a synchronous or asynchronous oral or written conversation, instructors can make good use of the oral asynchronous mode to guide learners in producing target forms and lexical items. The use of voice and intonation in this regard can be quite compelling – it is, after all, the voice in the live classroom that accomplishes this kind of corralling of learner output. The stretching out of the final syllable with question intonation in such a corralling prompt is quite common in English:

T: You turn right   at   ?

Using intonation, an instructor's corral could in effect be a cloze sentence:

T: So, you turn right at mmmm Street?

with the mmmm serving as the blank learners are corralled to complete.

Similar corralling audio posts can focus on pronunciation, syntax and clarification of learner comprehension. In the following description task, a learner's audio response indicates that she is struggling with pronouncing the English word *kitchen*.

S: You go living room into chichen. In chichen I see two window...
T: Kit – chen. Kit – chen. You go into　?

Again, by virtue of the oral asynchronous, the learner can repeat this teacher audio post as many times as she wishes and rehearse prior to recording and re-recording her corrected response. Because this is an audio file, she can also save it in a special folder that in this case she has entitled *Needs More Work*.

Saturating

A cornerstone of language learning, especially at beginning levels, is repetition. The more one encounters a form or lexical item in the target language, be it in written and/or aural form, the more likely one is to remember and incorporate that language into one's developing repertoire. A concomitant instructional conversation strategy for language education has thereby been to saturate instructional utterances and design instructional conversation tasks that saturate the learner with the targeted language of the moment. In oral asynchronous modes, instructors have ample time to generate oral plus written and visual posts that indeed accomplish this well. Not only can she saturate by oral repetition, but she can make both meaning and form triply redundant by incorporating multiple modalities as in the following example. Here low intermediate learners of ESL/EFL have been working on a themed module on things that one can and can't depend on. In the **task toolkit** is an ever expanding list of vocabulary items that describe such things:

> a politician
> a car salesman
> a real estate agent
> a weather forecast
> a bus schedule
> an electronic translator

Because these are new vocabulary items, the instructor makes a point to saturate her oral posts with these terms as in the following:

T:　Yes, you can't depend on a *bus schedule*. *Bus schedules* are almost always wrong. I have a *bus schedule* that I can't depend on to come to class. I know several people who have *bus schedules* they can't depend on. *Bus schedules* make them late for class and appointments. Which *bus schedule* do you use to come to class? Is your *bus schedule* correct?

The use of online resources can be truly creative. In Figure 49, an ESL instructor created a voice thread for students to use when practicing English pronunciation. She also provides an animated illustration of the song *You Brush Your Teeth*. The song itself is saturated with the phrase 'You brush your teeth'. The animated context makes the pronunciation task more relaxing and can free beginning level students from the embarrassment and anxiety often associated with pronunciation exercises.

T: When you wake up in the morning, it's a quarter to one
     And you want to have a little fun,
     You brush your teeth ch ch ch ch, ch ch ch ch...
     You brush your teeth ch ch ch ch, ch ch ch ch...
     When you wake up in the morning, it's a quarter to two
     And you want to find something to do,
     You brush your teeth ch ch ch ch, ch ch ch ch...
     You brush your teeth ch ch ch ch, ch ch ch ch... /.../

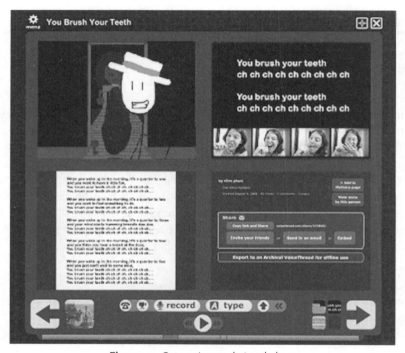

Figure 49 Saturating and visual clues

Saturation can very positively impact students' target language output. Students tend to notice the words and constructions that are repeated in messages especially when the words are given in their different forms and variants as in the following:

NNS: Hello everybody! The next topic is a *stress*. I guess the job market and private life can feel *stressful*. And I'd like to ask you a question. To reduce your *stress*, to not to be *stressed* all the time, what do you do? And how you cope with your *stress*?

Using linguistic traps

The oral asynchronous mode can be used effectively to trap learners into using the focal forms and lexis of a lesson or module. Instructor posts that respond both to meaning and to the learner's need to re-form their post to be phonologically, lexically or grammatically correct can be designed and recorded to this end. By trapping learners, we call their attention to the focal language and use instructional conversation in such a way as to force them to adjust their output accordingly. Again, the luxury of the asynchronous mode is the element of unlimited time: time for instructors to design effective traps, and time for learners to make use of instructor posts and other available resources online to refashion their responses using the correct language.

A simple generic audio post reminder to learners to: *Check the **task toolkit*** can serve as an effective trap that directs learner attention to the focal language they are to use productively. Other forms of traps can be to complete the phrase or sentence prompts that again make use of instructor intonation to signal the need for learners to supply the missing, required information thus trapping them into using the target language in the **task toolkit**.

Linguistic traps often take the form of questions asked in a way that 'traps' students in using only particular forms as in the next example. ESL students are asked questions that make it impossible to avoid using the present progressive form in their answers.

T: (*oral and written; page 1*) On the next pages you will see pictures of "actions in progress." Click the record button at the bottom center of the page to record your sentence. Describe what you see by saying a complete sentence using the present continuous form. There is an example on the next page (Figure 50).

Figure 50 Linguistic traps

T: (*oral and written; page 2*) What is the baby doing. He is sleeping. (Figure 51)

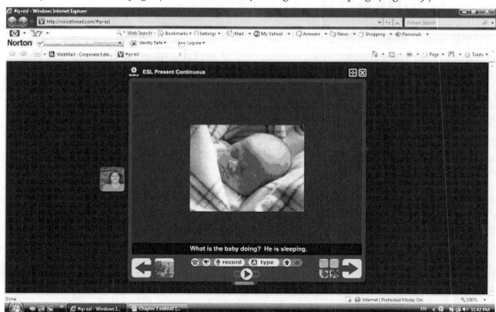

Figure 51 Linguistic traps

T: (*oral and written; page 3*) What is the girl doing?
S: (*oral*) The girl is skiing.

Modeling

Again, the oral asynchronous mode allows for as much time as instructors need to record models using their own voices, find and attach the voices and images of native speakers modeling the same targets, locate and add to modeled speech still and moving images that support comprehension and, in the case of pronunciation, adding cutaway images of vocalization and/or spectrographic images of the targeted language. Such multimodal posts can effectively model and even amplify the language currently under study. Posts to which learners may want to refer at a later time can of course be stored in the personal file folder of their choice for later review and reference.

To model authentic uses of the targets that appear in a **task toolkit**, in oral asynchronous modes instructors can enlist the voices of other speakers and engage in audio theater. If non-verbal gesturing is deemed key to a particular model, if the non-verbal behavior is particular to the target culture and not that of the learners, then video clips can be likewise fashioned and posted as models or simply located from internet video repositories. In the following, for example, the focal language for this ESL/EFL is language and culturally appropriate behavior (in this case, in the US) for apologizing for having forgotten something. A typical non-verbal behavior that accompanies verbal apologies is the open palms facing up and the shrugging of shoulders. Several video clips of native speakers apologizing while doing the 'palms up and shrug' are supplied as links from the **task toolkit** as models for apologizing in US English (Figure 52).

Video 1:   (*man*) My apologies...
Video 2:   (*man*) I'm very sorry!
Video 3:   (*woman*) Pardon me.
Video 4:   (*man*) Please forgive me.

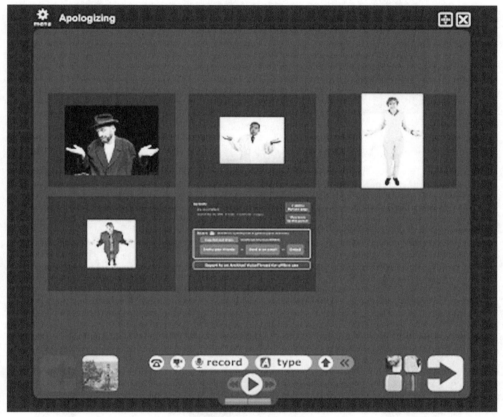

Figure 52 Visual modeling

Modeling can be accompanied with visuals, text and audios as in this example from an ESL lesson on describing people. At the beginning, the teacher provides students with a toolkit of face vocabulary and then models their use in a context.

T: (*oral; page 1*) Before we begin, let's have a quick review of face vocabulary. Here are many words that describe the face. Before I tell you the answers, take a few minutes to draw or say the meanings of the words. For instance, you could go "head" and then circle the head. Have fun. (Figure 53)

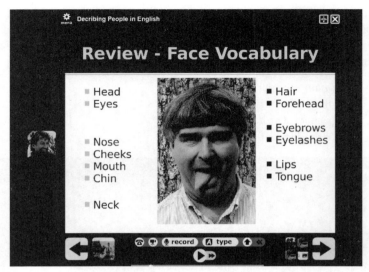

Figure 53 Modeling

T: (*oral, page 2*) All right. Now that you had a try, I'll tell you what the meanings of the words are. As I've already said, this is the head (*underscores the word and circles the appropriate part of the face as in Figure 54*).

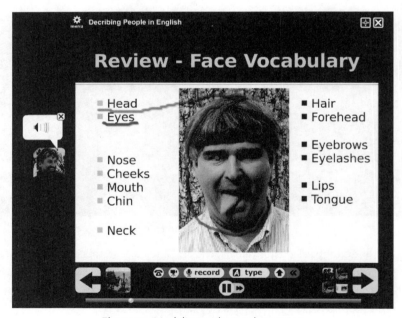

Figure 54 Modeling with visual attention

The teacher also provides **task toolkits** for describing eye color and hair as in Figures 55 and 56.

Figure 55 Modeling

T: (*oral*) Now I'm going to describe one of these two lively ladies. Silvia has straight brown hair and she has green eyes. Have you guessed yet? Now I'll tell you Silvia does not wear glasses. This is Silvia, right here. Now you should describe Kristina. This is Kristina.

Figure 56 Modeling

Providing explicit feedback

Like with oral synchronous modes, explicit feedback can be provided silently via visual markings and cues in oral asynchronous modes. In addition, instructors can incorporate pre-recorded explication posts about the focal forms and lexis. These can be inserted into the online conversations as they develop. Learners can opt to open these explanatory audio files while reviewing their and their classmates' online conversations. Additionally, these oral explanations can be accompanied by any number of supporting links and files; links to further explication, models and practice, files of the same. The beauty of this accessibility in asynchronous modes is that learners can select to attend to the kinds of explicit feedback they find most useful to them, be it aural, visual, textual, rules or examples.

Oral asynchronous environments are particularly well suited for explicit correction, considering the asynchronous and recorded nature of the medium when students can repeatedly listen to the instructor's postings, work more closely on their own utterances, distributing their attention to meaning and form more equally, and spend some time on reaching clarity on the use of new forms.

In a beginning level online Russian class, the assignment is to describe one's own physical appearance.

S: (*oral*) У меня есть коричневые волосы. Мои глаза тоже коричневые. [I have brown hair. My eyes are also brown.]

T: (*oral*) Джон, вы сказали, что у вас каштановые волосы и карие глаза. А какие глаза и какие волосы у вашей мамы? [John, you said you have chestnut hair and hazel eyes. What kind of eyes and hair does your mom have?]

S: (*written*) Is кареы [hazel] a better substitute for каречневиы [brown] when referring to eye color? (*oral*) Да, у меня есть каштановые волосы и карие глаза. У моей мамы голубые глаза и светлые и прямые волосы. [Yes, I have chestnut hair and hazel eyes. My mom has blue eyes and blonde straight hair.]

T: (*written*) Да, the adjective карий [hazel] (карие [hazel] for plural) refers to eyes ONLY. Russians do not normally say коричневые глаза [brown eyes] but карие глаза [hazel eyes]. By the same token, the adjective каштановые [chestnut] refers to hair only. You can't say каштановая ручка [chestnut pen] или карий карандаш [hazel pencil]. I'm glad you picked that up. Your next assignment is to describe a picture of a man (attached) and his physical appearance.

S: (*oral*) У этот мужчины есть серьга. У него есть карие глаза и каштановые волосы. [This man has an earring. He has hazel eyes and chestnut hair.]

As is exemplified here, oral asynchronous modes are excellent for explicit feedback as the class discussion continues on two levels, oral – for discussing the topic, and written – for an accompanying meaning negotiation. Thus, the main discussion can run smoothly in an oral mode, without visible interruptions.

As is reflected in the following example of a mid-beginning Spanish class, instructional conversations can be readily enhanced using explicit feedback with grammar notes, videos, audios, online exercises, etc. that can be easily viewed and accessed from the instructor's postings.

T: (*oral*) ¿Te gusta la cocina mexicana? ¿Qué te gusta en particular? [Do you like Mexican cuisine? What do you like in particular?]

S: (*oral*) Me gustan los tacos. ¡Los burritos es (*wrong verb*) buenos! ¡Y los burritos es (*wrong verb*) deliciosos! [I like tacos. They is (*wrong verb*) good. And burritos is (*wrong verb*) delicious.]

T: (*oral*) Me gustan los burritos también. Los burritos SON (*with emphasis*) deliciosos. [I like burritos too. Burritos ARE (*with emphasis*) delicious.] (*simultaneously provides a visual with the verb conjugations by adding a link to a grammar web site* http://www. learningspanishlikecrazy.com/Spanish_Grammar/Lesson007.html *as in Figure 57*)

T: (*written; in next turn*) Look at this video. It might give you more ideas about Mexican food. (*provides a link to a video from a web site* http://www.dailymotion.com/swf/x8s2m0 *as in Figure 58; students can view the video by clicking on the play button right on the screen; the video contains the grammar material in a context*)

T: (*written; in next turn*) Do this exercise (*provides a link to* http://www.spanishdaddy.com/ Tests/VerbLessons/SerVrsEstar.aspx *with an online self-check exercise on the use of Spanish verbs as in Figure 59*).

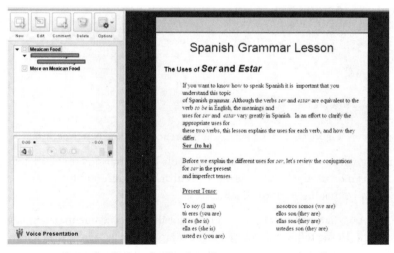

Figure 57 Explicit feedback. Reference to grammar rules

Figure 58 Explicit feedback. Reference to video materials on the web

Figure 59 Explicit feedback. Reference to online exercises

This example illustrates the numerous available tools (grammar notes, videos, audios and exercises) that can be used in layering explicit feedback into different forms and activities and, consequently, making it more effective.

Oral asynchronous, like oral synchronous allows for the use of iconic metalanguage in explicit feedback. In the following example from a Japanese class, an instructor provides a visual iconic representation of the concept of being animate/inanimate, critical in selecting correct grammatical structures in Japanese.

S1:   (*oral*) Mari-san no here nyu a? Nanik arimaska. [What is in Mari's room?]

S2:   (*oral*) Niko a um... arimas... [A cat is (*wrong verb*) there...]

T: (*written*) Be careful! Niko [cat] is alive, right, and moves around. So arimas [is] isn't the right verb. What is it then? (*simultaneously provides an animation of a moving person as in Figure 60*)

S2:   (*oral*) Uh... Imas? [Is (*correct but without a required subject mark*)]

T: (*oral*) Hai [Good]. In this case, Niko GA (*with emphasis*) imas [A cat IS (*with emphasis*) there], OK?

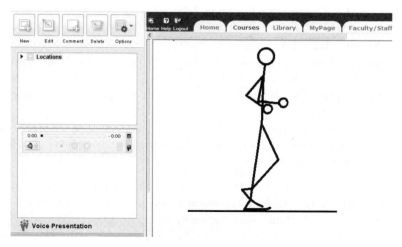

Figure 60 Explicit feedback

This example illustrates different forms for explicit feedback. The Japanese instructor uses the written mode in parallel with the oral conversation: corrections, notes, examples, references to Web sources, etc. He brings some elements of explicit correction into the oral mode only after the written feedback does not produce the correct output. His oral explicit feedback is partially in Japanese.

Providing implicit feedback

For many learners, explicit feedback provided in real time can derail the meaning quality of the target language utterances they are in the process of constructing. Thus, language educators often incorporate implicit feedback in what are otherwise conversational utterances as in the following ESL/EFL example:

T: Gene, what did you do yesterday?
S: Yesterday I pick flowers.
T: Oh, how nice! You pickED flowers, right? What else did you do?
S: I picked flowers. And I watched TV. Yeah... I watched TV.

The asynchronous and recorded nature of oral asynchronous environments allows for implicit feedback to be readily noticed by learners. Meaning/form-focused feedback (Table 1, pp. 53) is a common technique.

T: (oral) Здравствуйте. Расскажите о себе. Как вас зовут? Где вы живёте? Сколько вам лет? Где живут ваши мама и папа? [Hello. Tell about yourself. What is your name? Where do you live? How old are you? Where do your Mom and Dad live?]

S: (oral) Здравствуйте. Меня зовут Джон. Я играю гитара (*wrong ending; missed preposition*). Я живу в Колорадо. Мне 18 лет. Мою маму зовут Джессика, и моего папу зовут Пол. Они живут в Колорадо. [Hello. My name is John. I play guitar (*wrong ending; missed preposition*). I live in Colorado. I'm 18. My Mom's name is Jessica and my Dad's name is Paul. They live in Colorado.]

T: Здравствуйте, Джон. Вы играете только НА ГИТАРЕ (*with emphasis*)? А вы играет на рояле? Вы играете на барабане? У вас есть друг? На чём он играет? [Hello, John. Do you play guitar only? Do you play piano? Do you play drum? Do you have a friend? What does he play?]

S: Да, я играю только на гитаре. У меня есть друг. Его зовут Стив. Он играет на барабане. [Yes, I play guitar (*correct ending; correct preposition*) only. I have a friend. His name is Steve. He plays drums.]

In this example from a Russian class, the instructor gently corrects a student's mistake in the use of the phrase 'to play a musical instrument' and also engages him in a continuation of this asynchronous conversation by asking questions that model the correct use of the problematic construction. At the same time she 'traps' the student into using the correct form.

Summary

Comprehending naturally paced spoken language can be a challenge even in one's native language. In a new target language this is particularly challenging. The oral asynchronous mode is particularly supportive of comprehension in this regard. Audio files generated by instructors and those that are found material can be used to great advantage as primary and corrective models of the focal language. Instructor-generated oral posts have the distinct advantage of being tailored to the particular group and even student and can thus target learner utterances in ways that are conversational (authentic, meaning focused), personalized (incorporating shared information, students' names, etc.) and optimally instructional.

End of chapter notes

Free voice recording resources

http://voxopox.com

http://Audacity.com

http://vocaroo.com/

Center for Language Education Research (CLEAR)
http://clear.msu.edu/clear/

Center for Advanced Research on Language Acquisition (CARLA)
http://www.carla.umn.edu/

Free resources allowing for oral asynchronous communication

Oral asynchronous is a versatile environment. Among the four instructional venues, it allows for the largest mixture of integrated pieces of text, video and audio. It allows for combinations of languages, genres, cultures in the same virtual room. Using such free resources as, for example, VoiceThread at http://voicethread.com, instructors can create multilingual and multimodal threads. The thread moderator starts a discussion:

Participant 1: (*oral; in English*) Here is one of my avatars. I just wondered what do you think I'm like. You can answer in any language you want, you can answer in English, Spanish, French, German, Welsh, {Jidda}, whatever language you want. /.../ At the end is the picture of me. How'd you like to comment on my avatar. Do you like me or not (Figure 61)?

Figure 61 VoiceThread 1

Participant 2:   *(written; in English)* Hello Lisa. Hope this doesn't make people laugh at you too much... ;-) *(draws a mustache, a beard, and a nose on the avatar)* (Figure 62)

Figure 62 VoiceThread 2

Participant 3:   *(written; in Spanish)* En este foto tienes un flor en el pelo. ¡Cuidado con este toro! [In this photo you have a flower in your hair. Taken care of with this bull!] (Figure 63)

Figure 63 VoiceThread 3

Participant 4: (*oral; in English*) This is the avatar I most used to. So this is an avatar I mostly associate with you. (Figure 64)

Figure 64 VoiceThread 4

Participant 5: (*written*) Tha falt bàn air Lisa! (Figure 65)

Figure 65 VoiceThread 5

Participant 6:   (*video plus voice; in English*) Hi Lisa. Why do you think it's my favorite avatar? It might have something to do with this thing standing behind you (circles the bull on the picture) Do you see him there? This bull... It does not make me very scared. It must be a nice friendly bull like my Angus. (Figure 66)

Figure 66 VoiceThread 6

Participant 15:   (*written; in German*) Ich glaube, dass Sie gern singen. [I believe that you like to sing.] (Figure 67)

Figure 67 VoiceThread 8

Such a multilingual, multicultural, multiparty exercise can be useful for those trying to acquire more than one language simultaneously and/or those interested in different cultures and different perspectives on cultures, languages and interactions.

Combinations of online resources

Often several online resources become combined in the series of activities on the same topic: blogs and oral asynchronous, Second Life, oral synchronous, etc. Modern technologies allow for embedding different applications into one another to create unique opportunities and smooth transitions between resources. Teachers can take the best from each application and link them in the same activity to create the best opportunities for their students to observe, communicate and learn. Teachers who use blogs and Second Life as a basis for their assignments can also create subactivities for them in different modes. Some instructors call such combined activities 'mixers'. An ESL instructor conducts a blog for ESL learners on http://ellloblog.blogspot.com/ and embeds audio discussion activities from VoiceThread. Then, they create a voice discussion thread on the same topic on voxopop to which they provide links from it to their blog.

T: (*http://ellloblog.blogspot.com/search?updated-max=2009-06-02T16%3A53%3A00-06%3A00*) (*written*) I responded to everyone who commented on the voice thread. Thanks for participating! Click here to listen. (*the link is provided as in Figure 68*)

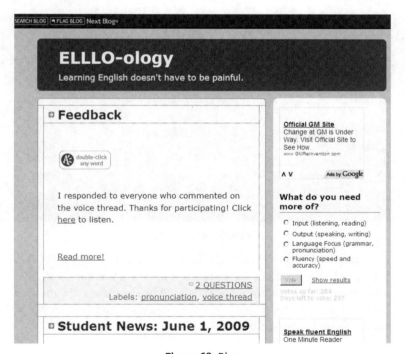

Figure 68 Blog

T: (clicking on the link brings learners to *http://voicethread.com/?#u85925.b513413.*
     i2736031 as in Figure 69) (*oral*) Hi. I've noticed on the survey I put up on the blog last
     week many of you responded that you need more output, more speaking in your
     English practice. So for Mixer # 90 this week I'm going to do a little experiment. I
     would like you to record short response into this page that you're seeing right now
     and for the first five people that recorded response I will give you some suggestions
     about your pronunciation and about your grammar so you can speak little bit better.
     OK, record a short response, 30 seconds or so, about how you stay in shape, what you
     do to exercise and I'll respond to the first five of you. (*written*) How often do you
     exercise? What do you like to do? How long do you usually work out? How do you
     stay motivated?

Figure 69 VoiceThread

T: (on *http://www.voxopop.com/group/01fabd9f-57c2-4246-a70f-596993e98e68*) (*written*) Go
     to mixer #90 at elllo.org to hear some samples of how to answer. (*oral*) We're doing a
     little experiment with a talkgroup discussion. I'd like to answer the question "How do
     you stay in shape?" another words how do you exercise? And you can find some
     samples to this on Mixer number 90.

Figure 70 Voxopop

Many language teachers who use Second Life start discussion threads on Voxopop and VoiceThread usually to clarify the meaning of common words or practice pronunciation (Figures 70–73).

Figure 71 VoiceThread and Second Life

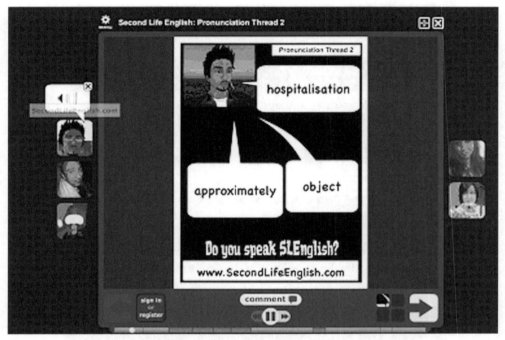

Figure 72 VoiceThread and Second Life

Figure 73 Voxopop

Combination of text and audio in oral asynchronous environments

As we have seen, participants in oral asynchronous environments often switch to the text mode to provide supplemental information or to steer focus on form or lexis.

T: (*oral*) Tea is usually drunk with breakfast...while eating breakfast. It is pronounced "chai" in English. That's easy word for us I guess. And the thing that the Turkish people like is the glass of this shape. Tea is drunk out of glass and it's a small wasted glass, in Turkish "engebelle bardak." And people put a little bit of sugar in their tea... it is... I don't know... tea is a little bitter I find. So that's pronounced "sheker" in Turkish. So the s with a cedilla is a "sh" sound, "sheker", and the c with the cedilla is the "ch" sound in "chai." Chai and sheker (Figure 74).

Figure 74 Combination of text and audio

T: (*written*) Hi, this isn't apple tea -I don't think so many Turkish people really drink that - more the tourists. Lots of people do drink freshly brewed herbal teas, like mountain thyme for the digestion. But at breakfast I see everyone drinking normal black tea. great question - thanks :)) (Figure 75)

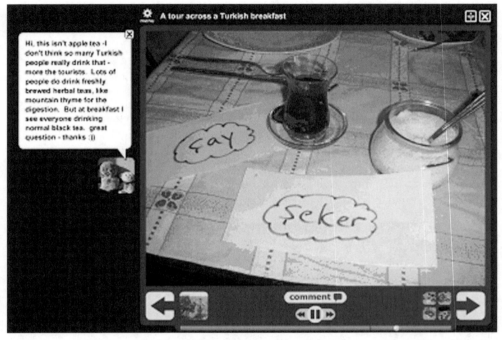

Figure 75 Combination of text and audio

End of chapter activities

Activity A. Injecting instructional conversation strategies

Look at the following transcript of English learners discussing test taking. With a partner, locate spaces within these conversation threads where oral asynchronous instructional posts might guide and/or redirect these learners to improve their English. Why do you think those particular instructional strategies would be effective in this context? Would you use oral or written modes for your instructional posts? Why?

Which eating utensils do you use in your country?

NNS1:   Hi everybody. Here is the topic. Which utensils do you use in your country? We, Japanese, all use chopsticks we call hassy when we eat something. Japanese food sushi and the other kind of food when we try to eat western food like spaghetti we change to the fork but some people like to eat spaghetti with a chopsticks. It is very funny. In my family we have all different chopsticks. My father has a long and kind of thick chopstick. And I and the other brother or sisters when we were kid we use shorter chopsticks. So each family member has their own chopsticks. And I like the chopsticks made of the bamboo or wood natural materials. I don't like plastic or iron things. So how about you? What kind of utensil do you use in your country? I hope to hear about that. Thank you.

NNS2: Hello. So in France no chopsticks at all (*laughing*). We just have the western utensils that are usually for the day meal fork knife and spoon. So they are made usually of metal do be more precise of aluminum in fact. But I want to say that when there are special meals special not special meals but festive dinner for example so that Christmas or if you go to prestigious restaurants, you'll see more utensils. So usually it's four forks, four knives, and one or two spoons. I'll try to explain it. In fact, you have a fork and a knife for the starter, a fork and a knife for the fish the fish plate and a fork and a knife for the meat, and a fork and a knife for the cheese. And sometimes we have a fifth one for the day sets. If you eat dessert, you ask for a knife and a fork. As for the spoon, you may have a spoon for if you have a soup to eat big spoon and have a small spoon for the dessert. And there is also usually three glass three glasses a glass for the red wine a glass for the white wine and a glass for water. So it's what you may find if you go to a prestigious restaurant.

NNS3: Hello to everyone. I have a question and wonder if NNS1 can reply to me. If I went in Japan at the restaurant I wonder if the waiter will ask me if I want to use fork, spoon or a knife. I'm just curious. Thank you. Bye.

NNS1: Hello NNS3. Your question is very very interesting to me. For foreigners and even for Japanese kid it is difficult to use a chopstick. You need time to practice chopstick. So when you visit Japanese restaurant you can ask the waiter to bring western utensils: a fork or spoon. Um... the most of Japanese waiters are nice to foreigners. So they don't think it's bad manner. So don't worry and ask them. Um... is it clear now? Thank you.

Activity B. Applying instructional strategies to the task

Analyze the following examples from an oral asynchronous discussion, identifying instructional conversation strategies you might use.

Is it easy to say 'I love you' in your country?

NNS1: (*written*) http://www.washingtonpost.com/wp-dyn/content/video/2007/11/21/VI2007112101814.html (*oral*) It give a very good idea of how difficult it is to say "I love you" for Japanese women. So I have posted the link to the video regarding this topic, and I would like to know if it is easy in your country to say "I love you" to your partner to show affection.

NNS2: (*oral*) It's definitely not easy for Finn to say "I love you." I think Finns often compare to Japanese. They are alike, little shy.

NNS3: (*oral*) It's the first time I hear that Japanese are compared to Finns. Usually Finns are compared to Swedes. Japanese are usually compared to Chinese, no? They have similar oriental cultures.

When you go to a restaurant what is the most important thing for you?

NNS1: When you go to a restaurant, what is the most important thing for you? I mean is the food the most important thing? Or the beverage is the most important things?

Or the waiter? Or the waiters are the most important things? Or may be the decoration the most important thing for you? I mean the decoration of the dish or the decoration of the place?

NNS2: The important thing for me is the taste of the food. Decorations and the waiters are not so important. But if the waiter is so rude I may be don't want to visit that restaurant. But food is the most important for me.

NNS3: Well I think the oldest sense that this kind of question would be you know the food but when I actually think about it, the most important thing for me the service and the atmosphere at the restaurant. Even if the food is not all that good, if the service is really great and the atmosphere is really good, you know I can still have very enjoyable time. Um... if you can get the food and the atmosphere and the service (*laughing*), obviously that's fantastic... but yeah that's the service and the atmosphere for me. When you go out to eat, you don't just going out for the food, you go out for the experience of being out. So that's sort of why I feel the way I do.

Activity C. Participating in the oral asynchronous discussion

Pretend that you are an ESL student. Using any available software or website for oral asynchronous communication, participate in a discussion on the topic *What is your Favorite Country to Travel to and Why?* Add at least two postings to it, each at least 20 seconds long. Discuss the reponses received.

Activity D. Analyzing instructional conversation strategies in oral asynchronous mode

Discuss the online conversation in which you participated in the previous activity. What instructional conversation strategies were used during this oral communication? What instructional conversation strategies appeared to be the most/least effective from your point of view? What factors have contributed to the degree of effectiveness of these instructional conversation strategies? In what situations and/or applying what instructional strategies did you switch to written mode? In what situations and/or applying what instructional strategies do you prefer to stay in the oral mode? Complete the matrices below.

Instructional strategies	Most effective	Least effective	Factors influenced
1			
2			
3			
4			
5			
6			
7			
8			

Instructional strategies	Situations	Oral mode	Written mode

Activity E. Creating a lesson plan

Create a lesson plan that would include an oral asynchronous discussion for the language you teach. Include tasks and activities that you see as suitable for this environment. Provide a rationale for your design.

Activity F. Analyzing lesson plans

Analyze your own lesson plan. How does the knowledge of the eight instructional conversation strategies you have learned about in this chapter and the affordances/limitations of the oral synchronous environment influence your way of organizing the materials, tasks and activities? Write a one-page reflection, answering these questions.

Activity G. Analyzing video, audio, and text in oral asynchronous environments

Investigate the threads on http://voicethread.com or another available voice discussion board, searching for educational activities in the language you teach or ESL. Find examples when the use of video, audio, and text is indeed instructionally effective. In what situations do you think those modes can be used interchangeably and why? In what situations do you think one mode has instructional advantages over the others and why?

Further reading

Blake, R. (2005) Bimodal CMC: The glue of language learning at a distance. *The Computer Assisted Language Instruction Consortium Journal* 22 (3), 497–511.

Ice, P., Curtis, R., Phillips, P. and Wells, J. (2007) Using asynchronous audio feedback to enhance teaching presence and students' sense of community. *Journal of Asynchronous Learning Networks* 11 (2), 3–25.

Volle, L. (2005) Analyzing oral skills in voice email and online interviews. *Language Learning Technology* 9 (3), 146–163.

4

Oral venues amplified via text and visuals

Chapter 4 summarizes the oral venues discussed in Chapters 2 and 3 and expands the notion of amplifying oral instruction using text and visuals. The following amplifications are discussed and illustrated:

- Non-intrusiveness
- Time savers and gatekeepers
- Salience
- Accessibility
- Familiarity

Oral venues amplified via text and visuals

In language teaching and learning, online instructional conversations in oral environments, both synchronous and asynchronous, are often amplified in two ways:

1. Oral communication is often supplemented with **textual** communication with voice being a primary means of communication while text is used in various ways to amplify the oral component.

2. Oral communication becomes highly **visualized**: images, symbols, emoticons, charts, arrows, circling, underscoring, videos, embedded visuals, etc.

Five factors can be viewed as influencing these two modes of amplification:

1. Text and visuals incorporated into oral venues make interruptions to conversations – potential interruptions such as comments, focus on form, requests of clarifications, summarizing, etc. – **less intrusive**. Indeed, their inclusion can be communicatively seamless.

2. Text and visuals included in oral venues serve as **time savers**. They make any digressions from the main topic of conversation economical. In addition, they can be useful in avoiding switching to students' native language and, therefore, can be used to function as **L2 gatekeepers**.

3. Text and visuals in oral venues make focus on meaning and focus on form more **salient**.

4. Unlike spoken words, text and visuals are **accessible**. It is impossible to review spontaneous oral speech in oral synchronous environments unless it is recorded and archived. On the contrary, text and visuals can be easily reviewed with a single mouse click.

5. Digital natives are quite fluent in these forms of multimodal communication. Their **familiarity** with text messaging and chatting creates a more comfortable and relaxed atmosphere during communication.

In oral modes of communication, text and visuals used in addition to voice can play different roles in the task:

- textual/visual task toolkits;

- duplicating oral messages;

- web links;

- summaries;

- emphasis;

- expressing emotions;

- clarifications;

- negotiation of meaning;

- focusing on meaning;

- focusing on form;

- additional comments on the topic;

- modeling;

- substituting oral postings with textual ones on the beginning stage.

Chat boxes, callouts, added comment functions and small pop up windows are usually the features through which oral modes are amplified with text. Emoticons, drawing, circling, underscoring, inserting shapes, adding images and embedding videos are common ways visuals can be used to supplement oral modes of instruction.

Non-intrusiveness

As the main focus of language education is on meaningful, real-life communication, one would assume that every digression from the topic, be it for focus on form, a question, a comment, an association or a summary, can be perceived by conversation participants as unnatural and intrusive to the point of being a conversation stopper. Teachers and students intuitively search for ways to make such digressions less disruptive. Focus on form, comprehension checks, commenting or redirecting in oral modes are often performed by switching to a different modality that is undisruptive to the main conversation.

In the following example from an oral synchronous portion of an online Russian class, students are asked to tell how good they are at certain activities, i.e. how well they speak Russian, play soccer, know US movies, etc. The students, engaged in a meaningful and fun task, feel quite relaxed conversing about themselves with one another. They laugh, make jokes and tease each other. In this situation, making explicit corrections could be perceived as intrusive and inhibiting to the generation and comprehension of meaning. Rather than halt the conversation, the instructor corrects a student very gently by using a visual (Figure 76).

S: (*oral*) Я плохо писать по-русски. [I badly to write (*infinitive instead of the first person*) in Russian.]

T: (*underscores the infinitive ending of the verb "to write"*)

S: (*oral*) Я плохо пишу по-русски. [I badly write (*correct ending*) in Russian.]

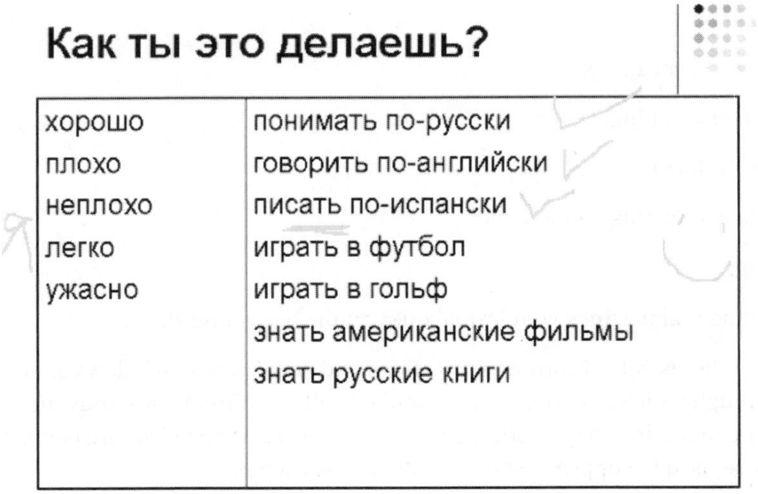

Как ты это делаешь?

хорошо	понимать по-русски
плохо	говорить по-английски
неплохо	писать по-испански
легко	играть в футбол
ужасно	играть в гольф
	знать американские фильмы
	знать русские книги

Figure 76 Oral venues with text and visuals. Non-intrusiveness

In the next example, students and their ESL teacher asynchronously discuss their attitudes about fast food in different cultures. While keeping the main discussion going, the teacher helps with lexis in the student's utterance by adding a short text comment.

S: (*oral*) In my country, we do not eat a whole lot of fast food. We usually cook home or go out to restaurants where we eat with families and friends. We usually eat a lot of pasta with bread and vegetables and... I forgot the word...

T: (*written*) spaghetti? (*oral*) Here the US people eat a lot of junk food unfortunately. We have chains of fast food restaurants such as McDonalds, KFC, and others.

Time savers and L2 gatekeepers

Time is an issue in any instructional environment. Nothing saves time more in oral communication modes than the use of visuals that function as symbolic, iconic, metaphoric or schematic representations of words. In the following example, a Russian instructor teaching in an oral synchronous environment uses symbols and drawings to keep the task going without spending time explaining to the students what was wrong in an utterance. Focus on form, thus, was performed very quickly without verbal interruption of the student's utterance and by switching to the native language (Figure 77).

S: Собака в кресле. [The dog is in the armchair.]

T: (*draws an armchair and a dog; shows with arrows that the dog can be on the armchair or inside of the armchair; draws a question mark*) В кресле? [In the armchair?]

S: (laughing) Собака ... **НА** (*with emphasis*) кресле. [The dog is on... **ON** (*with emphasis*) the armchair.]

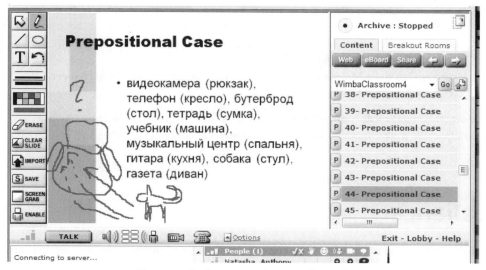

Figure 77 Oral venues with text and visuals

Text also can function as a time saver in oral asynchronous environments where students use text to express ideas that are not centrally relevant to the main conversation. In the text portion, they can make quick comments, for example. In an elementary German class, students are asked to tell about their families using celebrities instead of their family members. As annotation to a student's oral presentation, others put their written comments about the celebrities he was referring to (Figure 78).

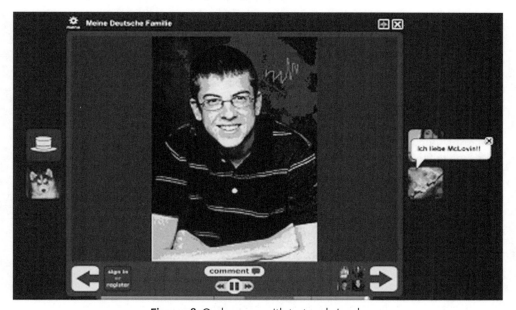

Figure 78 Oral venues with text and visuals

S1:   (*oral*) Mein Bruders Name ist McLovin. Er ist zwanzig Jahre alt. Sein Haar ist braun und kurz. Er hat braune Augen. [My brother's name is McLovin. He is twenty years old. His hair is brown and short. He has brown eyes.]

S2:   (*written*) Ich liebe McLovin auch! [I love McLovin too!]

S3:   (*written*) Ich liebe McLovin!! [I love McLovin!!] (*oral*) Das ist meine Schwester Ashley. [This is my sister Ashley.]

The target language text comments added to the oral messages help students practice the language skills in two modes, save time and avoid switching to L1.

Salience

Simply switching to another mode can also function as an attention getter. By using visuals and text, points can be emphasized and key ideas made more salient. For example, an ESL teacher starts a voice discussion thread 'How's the neighborhood where your family lives?' explaining the topic, providing directions and asking navigating questions in the oral part of his message. When he realizes that topic is not stimulating any conversation, he adds a voice message repeating his question while giving textual models of possible answers.

T: (*oral*) The question is how's the neighborhood where your family lives? Perhaps you would like to make a physical description of the street or the tower top building where you stay. Perhaps you can tell us a little bit about your neighbors, who your grandmother loves to talk with or maybe you don't know anybody in the neighborhood where you live. Describe as much as you can of your neighborhood and possibly your apartment or flat, the house where you live.

T: (*four days later*) (*oral*) What is it like where you live, where your family lives, or where you and your friends are? Tell us all about your neighborhood and your city or your town? (*written*) There are several cafés, food stores, stationery shops and a few pharmacies within 5 minutes walk in my rather quiet neighborhood.

Such textual models call attention to the task elements while prompting students to contribute to the voice discussion by following the model.

Text and visuals in oral synchronous environments can make focus on meaning or focus on form more salient without verbally pointing them out. In an activity about traveling to different sites, intermediate Russian students talk about different countries and states. The grammar focus of the activity is on the accusative case which is used in talking about destinations (Figure 79).

S: Я каждую неделю езжу в Атланта. [I drive to Atlanta (*incorrect use of the Nominative case ending instead of Accusative*) every week.]

T: Я каждую неделю езжу в Атланту. [I drive to Atlanta (*correct ending*) every week.] (*returns to the previous slide and circles the ending of the nouns in the model*)

S: Я каждую неделю езжу в Атланту. [I drive to Atlanta (*correct ending*) every week.]

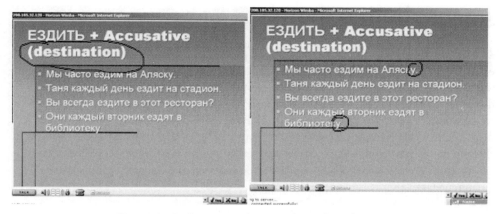

Figure 79 Oral venues with text and visuals. Salience

Such visually enhanced feedback has a better chance of being noticed by a student and consequently there is a better chance that learners will internalize what has been brought to their attention.

In the following example, a Japanese instructor while explaining the task, circles, underscores and brackets certain portions of phrases in his models to call students' attention to these visually while he speaks about them (Figure 80). Again, this renders focal language more noticeable.

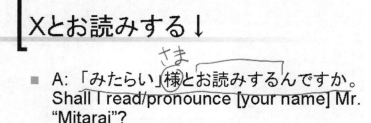

Figure 80 Oral venues with text and visuals. Salience

Accessibility

Text in oral modes is perfect for creating accessible focus on form elements. Students engaged in meaningful oral discussions, synchronous or asynchronous, can easily refer to text as review, as a reminder, or as a model. For example, in an oral asynchronous discussion, an ESL instructor explains the task 'Talk about what you did yesterday, last week etcetera using correct [-ed] pronunciation'. The pronunciation rule in its concise version is displayed in a comment box. Detailed comments can be read in a separate small window by clicking on the plus sign in the comment box (Figure 81). Thus, the brief pronunciation explanation serves as a **task toolkit** which can be accessed and referred to immediately during the task.

T: (*written*) [-ed] is pronounced three different ways depending on the last sound heard before the -ed. If the sound is voiceless, use [t]; if voiced, use [d]; but if the last sound IS a /t/ or /d/; use [Id] (*oral*) Today and perhaps tomorrow we will work on the past tense or the past participle –ed that is pronounced as a [t] as in walked, talked, picked. There are some different sounds there. What I'd like you all to do is to post something and tell what you did yesterday, last week, last month, or last year and use the past tense using [-ed] endings correctly.

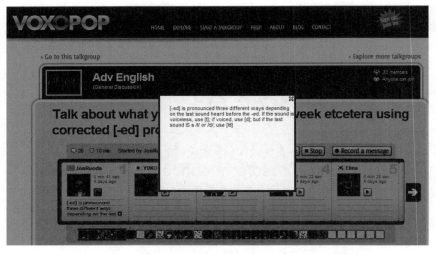

Figure 81 Oral venues with text and visuals. Accessibility

Such a technique allows for visualization of the rule that can be accessed at any time during the conversation. Moreover, the textual representation of the rule does not disrupt the voice discussion as focus on form is performed *on the side*. The discussion develops without deviation from meaning making.

The issue of comprehensibility is especially acute in oral synchronous environments with the fast pace and the lack of non-verbal cues such as gestures, face expression and eye movement. Text and visuals can be used productively to help overcome this problem. During an oral synchronous lesson, intermediate Russian students discussed things without which they would not be able to live (Figure 82). The grammatical focus of the activity was on the use of the genitive case after the preposition 'без' [without].

S: (*oral*) Я не могу жить... как по-русски TV? [I can't live without... how to say "TV" in Russian?] I forgot...

T: (*types the word "телевизор" [TV] in the chat box*)

S: Я не могу жить без телевизор. [I can't live without a TV (*uses the Nominative case ending instead of the Genitive case ending*).]

T: (*circles the word "без" [without] and draws arrows from it to the phrase "Родительный падеж" [Genitive case]*)

S: Я не могу жить без телевизора. [I can't live without a TV (*correct Genitive case ending*).]

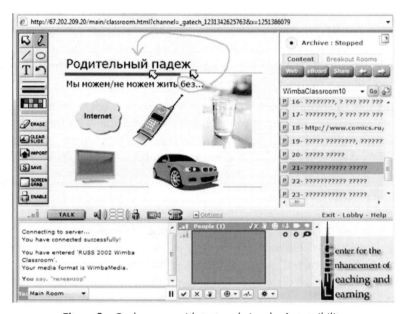

Figure 82 Oral venues with text and visuals. Accessibility

During the remainder of the oral discussion, both the textual representation of the word 'TV' and the visually augmented grammar rule are on the screen and can be referred to by the students at any time.

Familiarity

Digital natives are quite accustomed to text-based means of communication such as text-messaging and chatting and multiparty types of conversations. They are familiar with using text to quickly react to what is going on in oral communication even while maintaining more than one text-based conversation that parallels an oral discussion. Such side conversations when undertaken in the target language can be as beneficial as a main discussion. In the following oral synchronous class, the instructor and her students are discussing what is allowed and what is not allowed to be done in a classroom.

T: (*oral*) Можно читать книгу в виртуальном классе? [Is it allowed to read a book in a virtual class?]

S1: (*oral*) Нет... Да. Я не знаю. [No... Yes. I don't know.] It depends what book I guess (*laughing*).

S2: (*written*) Лори всегда читаеш Хари Поттер в классе ха ха [Laurie always reads Harry Potter in class ha ha]

S1: (*oral*) Можно читать учебник в классе. Нельзя читать не учебник [It is allowed to read a textbook in class. It is not allowed to read a non-textbook] (*laughing*). (*written*) джошь ы читаешь химия только :) [josh you read chemistry only :)]

Two students become engaged in a conversation entirely in Russian that goes on at the same time as the focal, teacher-led conversation. Communication in the target language in two modes simultaneously is enriching for students' language skills and helps develop their confidence and fluency in using the target language.

In oral asynchronous environments, participants develop a style of communication that combines oral messages with written comments in a way that allows for the quick browsing of oral messages. In the following oral asynchronous discussion students talk about how people in different cultures use body language and gestures to greet each other.

S1: (*oral*) In Germany, when we meet someone, we treat them with shaking hands. When we meet friends, they hug us.
(*written*) someone = shake hands   friends = hug

S2: (*oral*) In Brazil, it's different from place to place and it depends on the origin of the family but generally speaking I would say if you don't know a person, just shake the hands. And in the case of friends, you shake hand and give a hug but not for a woman. If this woman is your close friend, you shake her hand and give her three kisses on her face. Young people kiss all young people it doesn't matter if it's a man or a woman. In the case of two men, it depends on their relationship but ... well a man shake your hand and give a kiss on the face and in the case of for instance uncles and nephews or fathers and sons but in the case of the entire family you know they kiss everybody (*laughing*). (*written*) someone: shake hands   friends: shake hands + hug close woman friend: shake hands + 3 kisses (face)

Here text is used to schematically represent oral messages for fast browsing and for making the decision as to whether or not to listen to the whole message. It also conveniently summarizes the ideas represented in the thread.

The use of visuals to highlight the main points of oral messages is something to which digital natives are accustomed and can be provided immediately in the form of linked or embedded videos and images. For example, in the following oral asynchronous discussion thread about traditional dances and music, students provide links to YouTube videos, wikipedia articles and illustrations, and google images (Figure 83).

S: *(written)* www.youtube.com/watch?v=v5bwS62m_Sk&feature=related *(link to a YouTube video) (oral)* Here is the piece from Poland. This is a link to a real traditional Polish dance that is called Krakowiak. And you can see on this video where the famous dancing group performs it on the main street of Krakow.

Figure 83 Oral venues with text and visuals. Familiarity

This digital connection between oral speech, text and visuals allows students' ideas to be viewed in different modes simultaneously. This is something that needs to be incorporated into both traditional and online classrooms to make the best use of young people's everyday routine communication habits.

Summary

Oral online environments can be easily and effectively amplified with text and visuals to great pedagogical effect. Indeed, combining modalities in ways that make sense to digital natives in instructional formats is an important instructional technique that can be used to teach language well online.

5

Language learning and teaching in written synchronous environments

- Synchronous written environments and their special features and affordances are defined.

- Discussion and illustrations of the many ways effective instructional conversations can be employed in these environments are provided.

- The pros and cons of synchronicity in written environments are outlined.

Language learning and teaching in written synchronous environments

Objectives

In this chapter you will learn:

- the definition of written synchronous environments;
- the special affordances of written synchronous environments;
- how different instructional conversation strategies can be undertaken in these environments;
- how the environment's affordances can be taken advantage of to support and amplify these conversations.

Overview

Written synchronous environments are spaces where written exchanges take place in real time. Such real-time text exchanges fall under the names *chat* or *texting*. Interlocutors read and type messages often to more than one person at a time. Messages appear instantaneously on the receiver's screen with all language and typographical errors intact. Thus, in many ways written synchronous modes can be viewed as resembling real-time face-to-face (f2f) interaction in that these written messages can be just as linguistically messy as they are in live interaction. At the same time, for language learners written synchronous modes have potential benefits in that mutual meaning must be worked for or 'negotiated' and when understanding is absent, repairs must be made. In short, like in f2f talk, one must work and work hard in real time to assure shared comprehension. This kind of active negotiation work is widely considered a key element in new language development (Blake, 2000; Doughty & Long, 2003). Moreover, research on written synchronous modes used in language learning suggests that learners tend to pay increased attention to lexical production and comprehension than in live talk (Meskill & Anthony, 2005; Pellettieri, 2000; Smith, 2003). The affordances of written synchronous environments allow learners more time to reflect on their own output, which leads to the increased accuracy of their production (Smith, 2004).

The differences between f2f and written synchronous communication are, of course, important to note. First, because multiple posters are often posting, the threads of online conversations can often become tangled. The sequence or sequences of conversation tend to be scattered, not as linear as in asynchronous modes where time allows for targeted composing and posting. Thus, when orchestrating instructional conversation strategies, instructors must be aware that their real-time posts may appear not as adjacent turns, but in what may appear as random order. The good news, however, is that due to digital native multimodal literacy, contemporary learners are quite used to picking through multiple conversation threads and reconnecting where needed to make sense of longer discourse stretches. Indeed, digital cell phone natives are well known to carry on dozens of conversations simultaneously via texting. This form of multimodal literacy or *polyfocality*, attending to disparate messages and stringing them together to make sense, can be viewed as supportive of linguistic skill generally, and of learning new languages in particular (Jones, 2004). When skilled online language educators capitalize on learners' predispositions to conversationally multitask, the potential for the written synchronous mode to be one that enriches language development augments. Moreover, research is indicating that language learners tend to take control of the conversation, an excellent means of exercising one's voice in a new language (Sotillo, 2000).

In Chapters 2 and 4, language learners and their teacher used the chat feature while engaging in oral synchronous conferencing as a space in which to have side conversations, duplicate oral posts for clarification, and as a place for sundry forms of commentary. It was also pointed out that these written synchronous exchanges can be readily archived and referred back to by both learners and instructor as a means of review and planning next steps in target language development. This chapter builds on these affordances while elaborating, with examples of course, the kinds of instructional conversations that can be orchestrated in written synchronous environments.

Calling attention to forms

As was explored in previous chapters, in synchronous online environments, learners can experience and engage real-time communication in the target language with simultaneous visual and textual support. In written synchronous environments, instructors can take advantage of the visual, written exchanges to draw learners' attention to the focal forms and lexical items under study. Because this happens in real time, the calculus that instructors employ in making on the fly decisions about what language output to focus on and how to achieve this must activate rapidly just as it does in the live classroom. And, due to the less linear progression of synchronous discourse, this challenge is doubled by attending to and management of what could be several threads at once. Like in the live classroom, defining and maintaining a limited focus on both the topic of conversation and the focal language to be used can be instructionally powerful. In written synchronous environments learners and instructors can see a running record of the instructional conversations as they unfold. Instructors and learners can thereby visually refer to, repeat or modify what has been posted previously as a means of calling attention to focal forms.

Task-level attention to form

The design and orchestration of language learning tasks in written synchronous environments may in many ways resemble the design and orchestration of language learning tasks in f2f classrooms. A given period of time when students are to be online has been specified, and a task, or series of tasks in which all are to participate is laid out and learner roles assigned. As part of the task assignment, the focal language to be used is presented, discussed and made a permanent feature on students' screens, the **task toolkit**, throughout. In this way, students and instructor can refer to the focal language as part of the instructional conversations while planning for, undertaking and presenting the outcomes or products of their language learning tasks.

One quick and easy visual technique that can be used to great effect in written synchronous environments is the paste-in icon. These icons (Figure 84) can be used as shorthand for any number of conversational and/or instructional purposes. In the following example, the instructor uses the **task toolkit** icon as a signal to learners to refer back to the focal language in the box that appears continually on the screen. In this example, the students are beginning level learners of EFL grouped in threes. Their task is to develop a dinner menu that is culturally and individually sensitive to all members in the heterogeneous class. The focal language is the language of making, accepting and rejecting suggestions and count and non-count nouns. As she monitors the trios' conversations, the teacher notes an error and inserts the **task toolkit** icon, thus signaling the learners to review and rephrase. To reinforce her point, the teacher provides a link to the web page on countable and non-countable nouns.

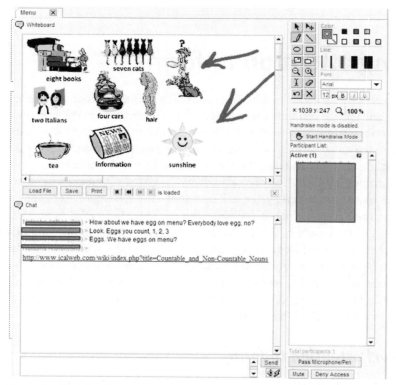

Figure 84 Task-level attention to form. Reference to representations of rules

S1:	How about we have egg on menu? Everybody love egg, no?
T:	▲ (*signals the students should refer to what was just posted and compare to task toolkit focal language by drawing the red arrows*)
S2:	Look. Eggs you count, 1, 2, 3
S1:	Eggs. We have eggs on menu?
T:	http://www.icalweb.com/wiki/index.php?title=Countable_and_Non-Countable_Nouns

The insertion of this or other icons that serve as signals to learners is a particularly useful technique in written synchronous venues as the insertion takes far less time than typing out explications, explications that can be readily accessed via links in the **task toolkit** if learners wish more clarification. If the inserted icon is overlooked, that is, the learners do not attend to the error(s) in their recent transcript, the icon can be reinserted and/or carry an accompany sound file and/or animate to draw learner attention. Of course, breaking into the conversation by posting a message that directly points out errors in learner posts, especially when those errors are the fixed focus of the particular task, is always an option. Additionally, because most written synchronous venues allow for access to multiple simultaneous conversations, the instructor can always 'take aside' a learner for remediation and explanation as needed. This, however, can be disruptive to real-time processes just as it is in the f2f classroom.

Task toolkits for written synchronous environments can be linked to or even embedded into blogs, chat boxes, personal websites, etc. An ESL instructor assigned the task 'What belongs to you?' with students directed to ask each other questions following the model: Is this X yours? Yes, it's mine. No, it's hers/his. The grammar focus of this activity was on possessive pronouns. The chat activity is linked to VoiceThread grammar material at http://voicethread.com/book.swf?b=154217 on personal and possessive pronouns that incorporates grammar notes with images, a voice lecture, a video with the song 'The Girl is Mine' by Michael Jackson and Paul McCartney, and the text of the song with all the possessive pronouns highlighted in a different color. During the activity, students refer to this resource by following the screen shot version of the grammar material on possessive pronouns or by following the link and manipulating the slides in VoiceThread to access the video and voice lecture (Figure 85).

This link allows the instructor to simplify her reference to the **task toolkit**. She can thereby mention the song, and students could easily follow her link.

S1:	Is this bag hers?
S2:	No, it's my.
T:	The giiiiiiirl is miiiiiiine..... la la la
S2:	oh yeah. The bag is mine.

Figure 85 Task-level attention to form. Reference to online resources

Incidental attention to forms

As learners use the language they are learning in written synchronous environments, the likelihood of their making mistakes in their posts is quite high. Granted, like all online environments, they have ready access to a nearly infinite number of supporting resources. In synchronous modes, however, as we have seen in Chapter 2, the pacing of communication often precludes hunting down the needed resource in real time. To overcome this, both teacher and students can keep ready links and files of their most commonly used resources right on their desktops to reference while participating in the synchronous conversation. Indeed, these kinds of selective resources can be information about forms, functions or pronunciations that a learner finds perennially problematic. For the instructor, based on prior live sessions, she too can select resources she knows will be most helpful to a given group of learners.

In the following example, an intermediate learner of French has continual problems with the gender of French nouns. With the coaching of his instructor, he is maintaining a spreadsheet of the masculine and feminine and neuter gender nouns (Figure 86) that he confronts and wishes to in turn use in his oral and written conversation practice as well as in the formal academic writing he is being asked to do in his content classes. A shortcut to this spreadsheet resides on his desktop so that he can continually add and refer to its items.

Figure 86 Incidental attention to forms. Reference to desktop resources

When playing an Association Game, students refer to this spreadsheet to use the proper articles.

S1:   la voiture [car]
S2:   le bruit [noise]
S3:   la pluie [rain]

A mid-beginning level learner of EFL easily mixes up English verbs that take the gerund (e.g. going) form only, those that take the infinitive form (e.g. to go), and those verbs that take both. On her own, she devised a text file that lists the three types of verbs. This she stores on her desktop and refers to often while participating in synchronous online class activities and while doing other kinds of target language writing. When her EFL instructor found out that this learner had devised this resource and strategy on her own, she asked the student to share it with the rest of the class. A few weeks into the term, all the students in the class were making use of this gerund/infinitive resource. Indeed, they even devised a special icon that anyone could insert into the online conversation to signal that the poster should reference it and in turn rephrase their post.

Incidental focus on form occurring in written synchronous environments can often take place as participants are correcting each other. To make focus on form more salient, participants use asterisks, capital letters and symbols.

P1:   Last year I signed in Economic university but I don't feel like I want to study economic...

P2:   (*to P1*) economics*

P3:   (*to P1*) why?

P1:   (*to P2*) thx...

P1:   (*to P3*) cuz I wanted to study architecture

http://www.easyenglish.com/esl-chat.asp

P1:   I onla know Hans Christian Anderson .....

P1:   or maybe one of the Brothers Grimm?

P2:   grimms were german, no?

P2:   anderson is dane

P1:   yes P2, they were german

P1:   P2 .... Was dane .... he is dead

P2:   WAS dane. right.

Studies suggest that learners notice such visual prompts and thereby make significantly more self-corrections than in the face-to-face environment (Lai & Zhao, 2006; Smith, 2004). Self-corrections in written synchronous environments usually take place during the second or even third turn which differs from f2f communication where if self-repair takes place, it is during the same turn when the error took place.

Calling attention to lexis

Whenever there is language teaching and learning in online environments, there are powerful opportunities to visually, aurally and contextually enhance student acquisition of new vocabulary. From initial comprehension of a new lexical item, to its nuanced integration in a learner-generated post, multimodal supports can greatly facilitate the process. In written synchronous environments, pictures, video clips and animations can be included in posts by both learners and instructors as a means of contextualizing and enlivening the meanings of new lexical items. Indeed, in the **task toolkit**, the venue for continued anchored referencing throughout a given language learning task, new and revived lexical items can have instructor- and student-generated links to previous contexts where the item was encountered, or to any number of related media.

Task-level attention to lexis

In the next example, advanced learners of French have been assigned to discuss the contexts and conversations at two French dinner table scenes, one from the film *Murmur of the Heart* by Louis Malle and the other from Renoir's *Rules of the Game*. After having simultaneously viewed and read the captions for each film clip, they are to introduce a point of comparison to which other learners respond. In her model for such a comparison and contrast discussion, the instructor uses highlighting in her text model to draw learner attention to some key lexical items that are specific to comparison and contrast, her end goal to guide learners in writing up formal essays using these same lexical items. These focal items are also continually present in the **task toolkit**.

As learners introduce and respond to one another's points of comparison, the instructor calls attention to correct use of these items by learners in their posts by cutting and pasting the learner's written utterance, pasting it in a subsequent message of her own with the correctly used lexical items highlighted.

S: Le scene de Malle est plus amusant de l'un de Renoir. [The scene in Malle's film is funnier .. the one in the Renoir film.]

T: Bien sur que the scene de Malle est plus amusant *que* l'un de Renoir. [For sure the Malle scene is funnier **than** the one in the Renoir film.]

S: Oiu cependent tout les deux sont comme meme un peu ridicule, no? [Yes, however they are both a bit ridiculous, right?]

T: D'accord. Autres choses? [I agree. Other things?]

In this example, a beginning level online Russian class works with vocabulary associated with making 'Russian Stuffed Cabbage'. Students engage in a series of activities such as listening to the audio and filling in the blanks in the dialogue with the words from the list, denoting ingredients for stuffed cabbage, watching the video on making stuffed cabbage, and a place maker interactive exercise. This exercise involves dragging the suggested ingredients to the image of the stuffed cabbage with the items that belong. The correct items (e.g. meat or rice) turn green. Incorrect items such as cucumbers or pears turn red (Figure 87). After that students are assigned to create a virtual stuffed cabbage by text chatting with each other.

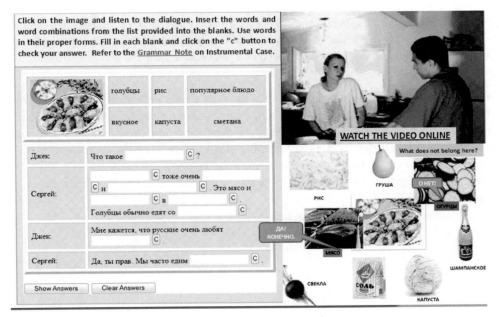

Figure 87 Task-level attention to lexis

During this series of activities, the emphasis is on the following vocabulary items (Figure 88):

рис	[rise]
мясо	[meat]
сметана	[sour cream]
капуста	[cabbage]
вкусный	[tasty]
соль	[salt]
голубцы	[stuffed cabbage]
блюдо	[dish]

Figure 88 Lexical resources

S1:   Надо брать рис и мясо. Фарш. [would need to take rice and meat. Ground meat.]
S2:   и сметана. [and sour cream]
S3:   нет, дрю. Сметана потом. [no, drew. Sour cream later.]
S2:   и соль. я не любью когда это нет соленой [and salt... I don't like when it's not salty]

An affordance of written synchronous environments is the real-time generation of ideas, albeit with the added affordance of unlimited access to information that might assist in generating those real-time ideas. An f2f pre-task technique, brainstorming a semantic net, is thereby an easily transferable technique for drawing attention to, and in the case of written synchronous venues, keeping a visual (and aural to be discussed further on) mapping of the lexical items likely to be useful for a given task. Either the instructor or one or more students can be designated scribe while the rest of the group generates a key word list for a given task in advance of undertaking it. Vocabulary items that all see as potentially relevant – this after exploring the items' meanings and their potential usefulness given the task requirements – are recorded by the scribe(s) and posted as a common document/file accessible throughout.

A class of high beginning learners of Spanish has started to brainstorm a lexical list for their upcoming task's **task toolkit**. The task is to role play two competing sides to a US Mexican border controversy regarding worker safety. As independent homework, students have read a number of news articles and viewed a number of video clips about the controversy in a particular border village that manufactures small engine parts. The students are given a semantic net (Figure 89) with Spanish (Mexican) words for safety, risks, health, accident, air quality, toxins, wages and regulations:

seguridad

riesgos

salud

accidente

qualidad del aire

toxinas

salarios

regulaciones

Figure 89 Lexical resources

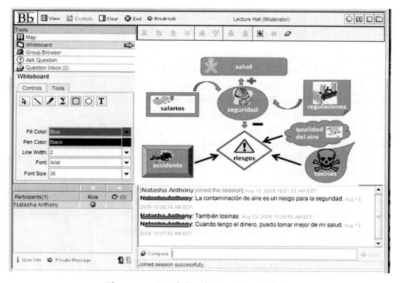

Figure 90 Task-level attention to lexis

Once the meanings for these vocabulary items are understood by all, be it by the participatory addition of links to visuals, examples of the words in use, or to translations, the group is divided into teams and undertakes the role play (Figure 90). During a subsequent synchronous class meeting, assigned learners will have reviewed the transcript of the role play, underlined the new vocabulary that was used and will then present this in a recycled version to the class as a form of review.

Incidental attention to lexis

Just as in the f2f classroom, opportunities for incidental uses and attempted uses of target language vocabulary are many. Like fast-paced live instruction whereby moment-by-moment instructional actions – drawing attention alternately to focal pronunciations, syntactic patterns, new or recycled vocabulary – while maintaining attention on the meaning value of all utterances is a complex juggling act and, as we have mentioned before, not all teachable moments can be detected and reacted to in optimal ways in the real-time messiness of human communication. Written synchronous modes can be just as frenetic and messy, but, given a running text record of all course interaction, those teachable moments are not entirely lost. At any point course transcripts can be revisited for any number of instructional purposes. When it comes to calling attention to incidental vocabulary – be it attempted uses of new words, use of words for which a more adequate substitute should have been employed, or as a general vocabulary review of items from a **task toolkit** used productively – teachers can make use of these for instructional materials and planning while encouraging learners to return to these transcripts and employ their best independent review strategies on them.

In the following example, a teacher of EFL directs her intermediate learners to use the transcript of language learning tasks they undertook several weeks ago and do the following as a form of vocabulary review in preparation for a midterm evaluation (Figure 91).

Directions for Midterm Vocabulary Review

Next week you will be taking your midterm examination. Included in this exam are the vocabulary items that have been part of our **task toolkits** that we have used in our learning tasks for the first six weeks of the course. I recommend that you review these __sessions__ (*link to location of course archives*). Depending on how you learn best, you can
- print these out and highlight the words you are less sure about
- make a cloze exercise for yourself by replacing words that are challenging with blanks then, at a later time, test yourself
- maintain a spreadsheet of the words you find difficult organizing by task, theme, or simply alphabetically
- if hearing the word helps you to remember, record (or have a native speaker friend record) it and play the audio and text files together
- if you wish to form informal study groups, you can share with one another novel sentences that you write using the new words as practice.

Figure 91 Review of **task toolkits**

Reviewing vocabulary items as they were productively used in familiar contexts is an excellent means of reinforcement while encouraging good independent study skills.

Negotiation of meaning can happen accidentally on the spur of the moment exactly the way it occurs in an f2f classroom.

P1: By the way, mr *P3* i think that you know *P5* the chatter from Sweden, one time he said "Oh my Thor" What's the meaning of Thor? Does it refers to the horns of the Vikings, because Thor means bull in Arabic .. or maybe he was kidding ?

P2: Thor is an old god

P3: P1: no, Thor is the Thunder God in Scandinavian mythology

In a multilingual chat room, incidental focus on lexis can take place not necessarily in a target language but in any other native language of the participants.

P1: I'm going too, have a nice chat all of you!

P2: Bye Mr P1, salam

P1:   salam

P3:   salam is bye?

P2:   Salam means Peace!!

Learners can be easily redirected to online resources: dictionaries, references, grammar notes, encyclopedias, thesauruses, etc.

P1:   Sasha is the Russian petname for Alexander

P2:   petname? do you mean a nickname? i'm not a pet he he

P3:   it is not a petname ..... it is the abbreviation of Alexander

P2:   P1, i believe the right way to say is "nickname" for a short name like Sasha for Alexander, Chris for Christina, etc

P3:   no .... nickname is a name that u choose ..... Sasha for Alecander ... it is the shortened version

P2:   oh so Sasha is the short version for Alexander, not a nickname?

P3:   no.... a nickname would be one that u choose ..... or that ur parents choose for u

P3:   or later your friends

P4:   not nikname, it short version

P2:   for example, Christopher is a full name, Chris is a short name, and "shorty" is a nickname, right?

T: It can be both a descriptive name and a short form of a personal name. Look at http://www.answers.com/topic/nickname. Listen to the pronunciation, too (Figure 92).

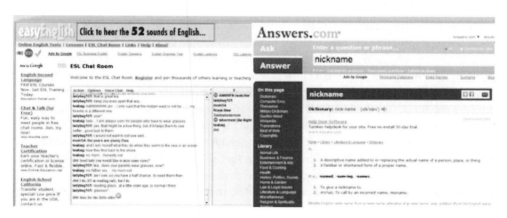

Figure 92 Incidental focus on lexis via online resources

Incidental attention to lexis is convenient in written synchronous environments as online dictionaries and other online sources are immediately available and can be opened in other windows. Chat aficionados are accustomed to doing this and include online resources often. They even take the initiative to share these sources and references with each other and their teachers.

P1:   i dont understand some words so i need online translater to use

P1:   (*later*) you're not allowed of pulling my legs, P2

P1:   allowed to*

P1:   allowed to pull*
P1:   leg pulling is forbidden in general
P2:   P1 .... it is generally forbidden with centipieds....
P2:   P1 is looking up the word centipied ...... lol
P1:   yep and figured out its meaning already

Another example:

S1:   what's up derek?
S2:   i'm mad at my roommate today.
S3:   derek is always mad or disgusted or unhappy... he's choleric
S2:   i'm not always mad... please... what is choleric means????
S3:   just a sec... let me open it ha ha
S3:   (provides a link to the web vocabulary video flash cards) http://www.wordahead.com/
        VocabularyVideos/Videos/TabId/59/VideoId/638/Default.aspx

Corralling

Task-level corralling

To review, task-level corralling entails a conversation move or moves that needs to be redirected to accomplish the dual tasks of fulfilling the requirements of the language learning task at hand, and using the target items in the **task toolkit** in meeting those requirements. It is an instructional conversation strategy that succeeds in redirecting learner conversation to a targeted piece or aspect of the language, and/or the task momentum and direction per se. Due to the fast pace of written synchronous environments, opportunities to corral students, while more difficult to determine than in asynchronous environments, abound as more real-time spontaneity tends to mean less focused, well-composed posts. In the following scenario, a teacher of intermediate French notes that a group of students' conversation is beginning to deviate unproductively from the task and its language objectives. Where the task is to compile survey data they had earlier collected asynchronously from native speaker counterparts concerning their likes and dislikes of popular culture, this group of students has begun to stray into territory unrelated to the task at hand.

S1:   Mais ma soeur aime bien les types qui s'habitent comme ca. [But my sister likes guys who dress like that.]
S2:   Zoot. La mienne aussi. Qu'est-ce qu'elles ont? [Mine too. What's up with that?]

The teacher joins the conversation instructionally and corrals the students into commenting on the native speakers they surveyed, not the tastes of certain of their family members, while simultaneously corralling use of a key **task toolkit** item, the verb *preferer*.

T: Donc, les genes francais qui vous avez demandez? Ils preferent....? [So, the native French who you asked, they prefer...?]

She thus redirects learner output, she corrals learners, to make use of a focal form for the assigned task.

In the following example, ESL learners work on vocabulary items for the topic 'Poverty'. They read online resources such as newspaper articles on the topic, grammar notes and interactive exercises on http://www.carmenlu.com/third/vocabulary/relationships3/poverty3_1.htm (Figure 93). Students then participate in a discussion on the topic 'Is poverty inevitable?' The following lexis is in focus: unemployment, poverty, hunger, famine, homeless, etc. Some students digress from the topic, and the instructor uses corralling to get them back on track.

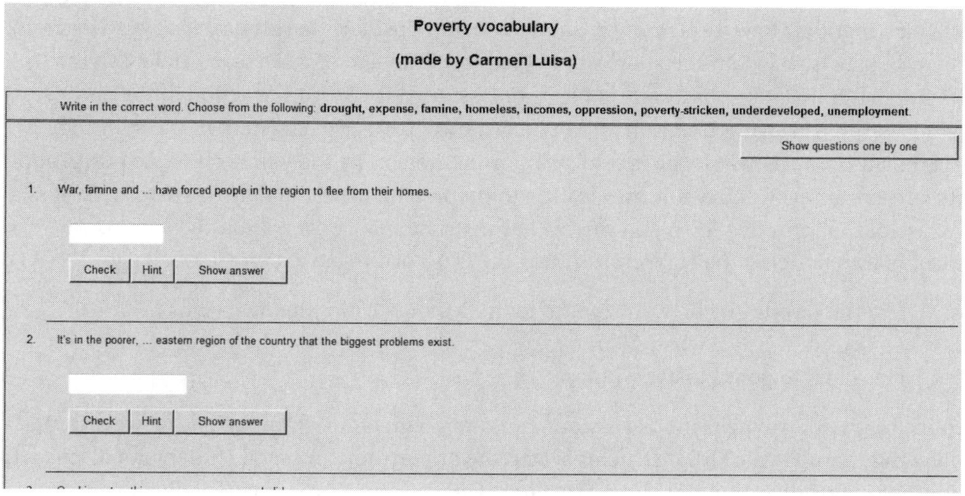

Poverty vocabulary

(made by Carmen Luisa)

Write in the correct word. Choose from the following: drought, expense, famine, homeless, incomes, oppression, poverty-stricken, underdeveloped, unemployment.

Show questions one by one

1. War, famine and ... have forced people in the region to flee from their homes.

Check | Hint | Show answer

2. It's in the poorer, ... eastern region of the country that the biggest problems exist.

Check | Hint | Show answer

Figure 93 Task-level corralling

S1:   the half people of planet cant cant have a bread to eat

S1:   and look where the money goes

S2:   Ann ... wrong again.. two thirds of this world's polulation don't have more than one meal per day

S3:   2 thirds ? wow, that is somewhat of an exaggeration

S4:   i have one meal per day for most the time. it doesn't mean i'm in poverty... it's just i don't have time... and simetimes i simply not hungry

S1:   oh you always say that tim but i saw you eat sandwich the other day

T: OK, Tim. That is your own choice to have one meal per day. What about people who do not have choices? What about unemployed people?

Incidental corralling

As we have said a number of times, truly excellent language teaching is determined by an instructor's awareness and subsequent exploitation of the myriad teachable moments that crop up in any language learning environment. No less the case are written synchronous environments where, under the pressure of semi-real time, learners are more apt to trip up and make real-time errors much as they do in live classrooms. Detecting just which slip ups are merely a matter of careless typing – for some, typing under time pressure can be daunting – or whether the way a target language item was used was a matter of faulty or lack of prior learning, is critical. This is again where archived **task toolkits** are useful instructional tools for decisions as to whether or not to corral learners into using something they have previously encountered and for which they have in the past been held accountable. Indeed, we have found that actively using and maintaining awareness of what is in the **task toolkit** archives can even bring other learners to take charge of the corralling that needs to happen to redirect learners to language that should be making its way into their repertoires.

In this example of incidental corralling, high beginning learners of ESL are rehearsing a role play that they have been assigned to record and post for the rest of the class to listen to. The role play is based on the short story, *The Man Who Shouted Teresa*, by Italo Calvino in the English translation. Each group has been assigned to sketch the action of the short story using a simple drawing program and to record their parts as characters in the story. The assembled products will be posted to and commented on by the whole class. As one group uses synchronous written communication to prepare their product, the instructor notices a misuse of the infinitive form and inserts her instructional conversation move to corral learners into noticing the correct form that the class had reviewed only a week ago.

S1:   That guy, your guy he wants go up to the window with others.
T: Your guys wants ...what? Wants to ...?
S1:   He wants to go up to the window.

Corralling written synchronous sessions can often happen in a playful, joking way. In the following example, an ESL instructor seized the opportunity to corral students to discuss the different words denoting the idea of stealing. The topic appeared accidentally during the discussion on a different topic, and the instructor used the situation to reinforce knowledge of these lexical items that had been on the radar in previous lessons.

P1:   P2 always writes in the burglarlanguage.
P1:   burglar´s tongue?
P2:   burglarlanguage ..... huhhhh what is this?
P2:   burglar is the one who robs houses
P1:   long time I had my last sausage stolen from the neighbor's fridge
P1:   I didn't burgle anything P2, how do you come to think that?
P3:   P1 talking about stealing...
P3:   i had a burglars steal my cash and laptop
T: P3, were there several burglars or just one?
P3:   oops... just one... a burglar
P1:   what happened to P3 now? Is she burgling her neighbor's fridge again? in order to serve us some sausages?
T: why do you say 'burgling' about the fridge? because it was locked, no?
P1:   ooops P4, recently P3 has stolen her neighbor's fridge key. loooool
T: if he stole a key and unlocked the fridge, then yes he is a burglar
P3:   u got a locked fridge?
P2:   T .... if he unlocks the cage where we are sitting in ...... we might be free ..... is he a burglar then too?

T: if he got the hot dog from an open fridge while his neighbor was sleeping, he is a thief

T: if he took it from him by force, it's a robbery

P2:   but P1 didn't steal while his neighbor slept .... he locked his neighbor in a wardrobe and took the sausage out of the fridge

P1:   P2 if he wants to steal us, he is a terrorist hahaha

P2:   and when his neighbor fainted in the wardrobe he took the second sausage

T: P2 then it's a robbery perhaps

T: if he opened the cage and freed us, he is a rescuer

P2:   no T .... inside the cage we were fed and had a place to sleep ..... outside we have to earn money for these

P1:   ok, then he is a revolutionary.

T: a burglar breaks into your house, a robber seizes things from you, and a thief steals stuff from your pocket secretly

Saturating

Saturating – making use of target words and forms as often as possible as an instructional conversation technique – works quite nicely in asynchronous written contexts as the repeated words and phrases can be inserted and reinserted into the stream of any real-time activity for review and reinforcement. Indeed, not only the instructor but others designated by the instructor can engage in saturating the running conversation with targets from the current and/or previously studied **task toolkits**.

In an intermediate French class, the instructor has noted that her students are using clever strategies to avoid using the passé composé, a challenging past form for English speakers. As part of a general discussion about first the travels of famous adventurers and then to students' own experiences traveling, she purposely saturates her end of the instructional conversation with actions in the past that take this particular form.

T: Alors, et nous savons bien que les genes qu'*ont voyagé* souvant son plus savant. Ils *ont* plus *vu*, ils *ont éprouvé* plus, ils *ont compris* le monde de diverses perspectives, ils *ont parlé* à beaucoup de personnes différentes... [Now we know well that people who *have traveled* are wiser. They *have seen* more, they *have experienced* more, they *have understood* the world from various perspectives, they *have spoken* with different people...]

In turn, learners are encouraged to use this verb tense in their own discussions of their travels and adventurers.

Saturation in written synchronous environments can occur simultaneously in several media channels: text in a synchronous chat, text and static visuals in the whiteboard area, and links to video and audio clips. Saturation, thus, becomes multimodal.

An ESL instructor prepares students for the chat activity on the topic 'Safe Flight'. Certain vocabulary items pertaining to this topic such as safe, safety, taking off, landing, luggage, baggage, booking the flight, checking in, etc. saturate both the instructor's initial message and the texts in all the sources to which students are directed.

T: (*written*) When you hear "Have a *safe* flight," what does it mean for you? What does it mean to be *safe* on a plane? Do you feel secure when you fly? For ideas, check this (*link*) **youtube safety demo video** and this (*link*) **blog**.
    (*blog*) (*written*) Being *safe* on a plane has a lot to do with karma. /.../ When the attendants start the in flight *safety* program, it's important to first put your seatbelt on and then listen to their performance with the utmost attention.
    (*youtube video*) (*oral*) We want to get you to your destination with comfort and *safety*. /.../ Before we take off, familiarize yourself with the *safety* procedures. (Figure 94)

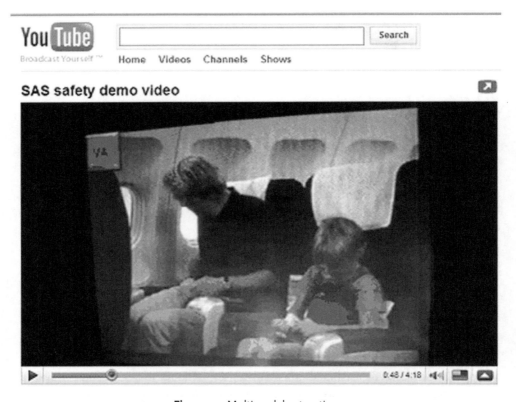

Figure 94 Multimodal saturation

Using linguistic traps

In written synchronous environments, while the pacing can be quite fast, both instructor and learners have the luxury of the text on the screen that can be read and reread as many times as needed. For the instructor, this means that learners need to attend to her instructional moves. And, as mentioned earlier, if her instructional moves get overlooked in the real-time messiness of synchronous communication, then she can always copy her prior posts and reinsert them into the text as many times as necessary to achieve her instructional aims. She can also fashion her posts into the kinds of linguistic traps that force learners to attend to and, in turn, produce the targeted language for the given task. In the following example, an EFL teacher is leading her mid-beginning learners in a role play whose focus is to ask, accept or reject a favor (Figure 95). The **task toolkit** can be seen in Figure 96.

Asking
Can you please...?
Is it possible that you could...?
I need a favor. Could you possibly...?

Accepting
Sure. No problem.
Yes, I'd be happy to.
Absolutely. My pleasure.

Rejecting
I'm sorry, but I can't
Sorry, but that's impossible.
Not this time, maybe next time.

Figure 95 Task toolkit

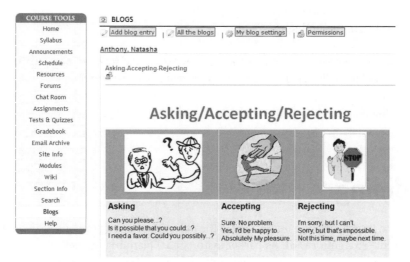

Figure 96 Using linguistic traps

Learners are working in a jigsaw configuration whereby each has a different list of favors to ask the others. The goal is for each student to get one 'yes' and one 'no' for each favor asked in order to complete their asking favors assignment. As the instructor monitors, she notes that one learner is having difficulty with the proper verb form to follow the English model (the infinitive minus the 'to'). She enters the conversation and traps the learner into using the correct verb form.

S: Can you to give me ride to airport?
T: Can you...?
S: Can you to give..
T: Can you...? (*inserts her symbol to check the* **task toolkit**) ⚙
S: Can you give me ride?
T: A ride.
S: Can you give me a ride to airport?
T: THE airport. Again.
S: Can you give me a ride to the airport?
T: Bravo!

Note: because this instructional communication is taking place by typing, the chances for typographical errors are strong. Detecting teachable moments such as the preceding one is confounded by the chance of mistyping.

The written synchronous environment is extremely dynamic. Communication happens rapidly among several participants. In addition, if allowed, some participants simultaneously chat with each other individually. Under these conditions, linguistic traps, usually more noticeable in other modes, can be less salient. Through the use of textual attention getters and repetitions, teachers can trap students into using target forms as in this example from an ESL chat activity on their country of origin.

S: i'm from philippines. i never leave any where
S: just here in philippines :(
T: So you live in the Philippines, right?
S: yeah
T: You have never **left** (*in a different font size, color, face, and style*) your country or you have never **lived** (*in a different font size, color, face, and style*) anywhere?
S: never left
S: right thanks

Modeling

Modeling the target language output that is the objective of a synchronous written online activity is quite straightforward. As part of instructional planning, model monologs, dialogs or group conversations can be composed or copied from a textbook or other source well in advance of the actual real-time online meeting. As part of the instructional conversation during the model-focused task, all or portions of the model can then be referred to by inserting an icon that indicates learners should consult the model, or a link from the instructional conversation directly to the model that appears in a pop-up window.

One variation is to assign learners to either develop or locate models of native speaker interactions or specific genres of writing around which instructional tasks can also be generated. Scripts of video clips, films and popular songs are particularly motivating in this regard. For example, an advanced ESL class was assigned to watch a US movie on their own. One of the students found a clip from the movie on the internet and transcribed it. She presented the clip and a cloze listening exercise with which she asked her classmates to practice listening and then repeating lines from the movie. Another student assigned the group the task of composing a letter to one of the movies' characters in which they were to use language similar to that in the movie itself.

Modeling in written synchronous mode often involves the instructors taking the role of one of the interlocutors in a task to get the conversation started. She thus sets the model and thus the target linguistic output for the task (Ene *et al.*, 2005). The following is an example from a beginning German class.

T: Ich heiße Jay. [My name is Jay.]
S: Ich heiße Lidia. [My name is Lidia.]
T: Ich wohne in New York. [I live in New York.]
S;   Ich wohne in New York auch. [I live in new York too.]

As with the other instructional conversation strategies, modeling can be performed in several different communication channels. For the chat activity 'What were you doing during our class meeting yesterday?' an ESL instructor models the use of the simple and progressive past tense forms for students in different modes: in her own utterance and in the embedded references to the instructional mini-video available online at http://www.geocities.com/hklo.rm/ (Figure 97).

T: (*written*) What were you doing yesterday during our virtual class meeting? I know that Lina was smoking. She told us :) I was looking at the screen all the time and talking. I was explaining the rule when my cell phone rang. You heard it, right? For models on using the correct verb forms, watch this (*link*) cartoon. For more examples go to http://www.whitesmoke.com/past-progressive-tense.html.

Figure 97 Multimodal modeling

Providing explicit feedback

As we have seen, synchronous written contexts are excellent venues for seeing and addressing aspects of learner posts in the target language. One of the instructional conversation strategies that works particularly well in this environment is to provide explicit feedback to learners by way of referring to course resources that have been assembled well in advance of synchronous meetings as part of overall planning. These resources can consist of the **task toolkit**, of course, and other reference material that instructors can make use of to explicitly direct attention and that learners can use in composing their posts on the fly. Reference to them can be via an icon, a link made directly within the ongoing course conversation, or as a private aside to a struggling learner.

In this next example of intermediate learners of Spanish, the instructor is quite aware, having reviewed archived transcripts of prior sessions, that a number of students still struggle with verb conjugations. She has therefore assembled quick reference files of conjugations for the different verb endings for which she can insert a link as in the following:

S1: ¿Adónde fueron? [Where did they go?]
S2: Ellos fue a la tienda. [They .. to the store.]
T: Third person plural, simple past >>link to conjugation file
S: OK. Ellos fueron a la tienda. [OK. They went to the store.]
T: Magnifico! [Magnificent!]

In the next example of beginning learners of Russian, the instructor incorporates visual, and thereby highly explicit and attention-getting feedback.

S: On January I was in Georgia. I was to visit my grandparents.
T: *(circles the word "Prepositions" on the whiteboard)*
S: On February I was here because I had to go back to the school.
T: *(draws an arrow pointed towards the preposition "in" on the whiteboard)*
S: In March?
T: *(draws a smiley face in the chat area)* :))))))))))))))))))) In March... That's right. (Figure 98)

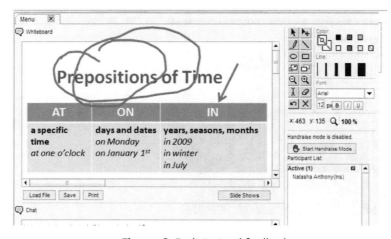

Figure 98 Explicit visual feedback

Providing implicit feedback

Where providing explicit feedback is an expeditious and effective technique, especially at the lower proficiency levels, implicit feedback can be less intrusive and work to keep the conversation on track in terms of its meaning exchange. The goal of using implicit feedback in a synchronous learning environment is to draw learner attention to an aspect of the target language and to do so while avoiding breakdown or distraction from the ongoing monolog or conversation. These implicit forms – highlighting, recasting or echoing – can work nicely in written synchronous environments. Unlike more explicit strategies, learners can always choose to ignore implicit feedback and continue on with their communication as is. And, if and when this happens, teachers can always make use of the archived version of the conversation as teaching material for a subsequent meeting.

Recasts

Because of the real-time aspect of synchronous written environments, recasts are a natural, straightforward strategy. Rather than taking the time to analyze and calculate an appropriate instructional conversation strategy that involves several steps, a recast – simply restating what the learner has written with a question mark – puts the ball in the learner's court as well as in the court of other classmates who are participating in the conversation. In this example, advanced learners of French are discussing a short story that they have read for homework. One of the students offers her opinion concerning a character's actions, but misuses a French–English cognate or faux amis.

S: À mon pense elle devrait être restée à partir de lui. [In my thought she should have stayed away from him.]
T: A votre quoi?? [In your what??]
S: Excusez-moi A mon avis. [Excuse me. In my opinion]]

Visual amplification of recasts in written synchronous modes can also be effective in attracting student attention. Capital letters, different colors, font change, emoticons, asterisks and other visuals can be used with positive effect.

S: I had lived in Albany for three years.
T: Do you still live in Albany?
S: Yes.
T: (*in red and bold*) ***I have lived in Albany for three years.***

Recent studies suggest that recasts in written synchronous environments should be not only visually enhanced but also followed by a metalinguistic comment or explanation to be more effective (Lluna-Mateu, 2006).

S: Yesterday I ***drink*** too much coffee and could not sleep.
T: Yesterday I (*capitalized*) ***DRANK*** too much coffee. ***Past tense*** :)
S: I drank. Thanks.

Meaning/Form-focused feedback

Non-native speakers in shared communities can implicitly correct each other during text chat activities as in this example, where two NNS chat via the Rosetta Stone SharedTalk web site (Figure 99).

Figure 99 Meaning/form-focused feedback

P1:   do you speak english fluently?

P2:   i am trying ;)

P2:   you can *juge* me

P1:   I can't *judge* you :) i'm not a native english speaker myself :)

To make meaning/form-focused feedback more prominent, instructors use visual strategies thereby increasing visibility and noticeability.

S: I worked in American company.

T: For how long did you work in an American company?

S: Actually it wasn't a real job. I had training in American company.

T: Was it (*asterisks*) *an* American company or a multicultural company? I used to work in a multicultural company with Americans, Russians, and Swedes.

S: It was an American company but we had people from many countries. Mostly Finns...

Echoing

As in the other instructional modes, echoing can be used effectively to draw learner attention to an error as an invitation to correct their post. In the next example of an informal conversation between a potential learner–instructor of French, the instructor echoes the learner's error to draw attention to it.

S1:   French is such a hard language to learn.

S2:   yeah sure but I can *learn* you if you whish

S1:   *I can learn you???* How can you learn me? I'm not a subject to be learnt he he

S2:   What do you mean?

S1:   Will you ***teach*** me French?

S2:   o yea I see... I'll teach you. oui :)

Summary

As we have seen with synchronous oral environments, there are certainly advantages and disadvantages to the real-time aspect of teaching online. This environment especially requires a great deal of pre-planning to ensure that the value of real-time communicative activity is fully exploited. Pre-planning involves anticipating the kinds of references and resources that can be made use of by both the instructor and students as they participate in task-based language practice accompanied by instructional conversations that are orchestrated by the teacher. While teaching, these resources and references can be called up, pointed out, referred to and used productively as learners compose their target language posts. Archives of these written synchronous sessions in turn make for excellent planning information and material for subsequent learning sessions and assignments. The most challenging aspect of synchronous online teaching, of course, is the element of time. Just like in the f2f classroom, instructors must juggle a number of instructional activities and conversations simultaneously while detecting and responding to the myriad teachable moments that arise. With practice on the part of students and instructor, however, the environment is a powerful one for language education.

End of chapter notes

My Language Exchange http://www.mylanguageexchange.com/Learn-Languages.asp
Shared Talk http://www.sharedtalk.com/
English Club http://www.englishclub.com/esl-chat/index.htm
Dave's ESL Café http://host8.123flashchat.com/eslcafe/
ESL Depot http://www.esldepot.com/page.php?xPage=esl-chat.html

End of chapter activities

Activity A. Task development

Taking the template on page 4, with a partner decide on a group of target learners, a language learning objective and develop a synchronous written task. Share your task with the group.

Activity B. Telling the story

Learners need not post only text messages in written synchronous environments. They can be assigned in advance of real-time online sessions to assemble multimodal presentations to share with the class. Indeed, these products – animations, video clips, audio clips and images in any combination – can serve as springboards for engaged discussion among class members. Visit the Digital Storytelling Project for ideas about assigning such multimodal storytelling projects. http://www.storycenter.org/index1.html

Activity C. Clozing video

As mentioned earlier in this chapter, learners can be assigned to transcribe a video clip that they find on the internet. Not only is transcribing in the target language a powerful language learning activity, but transforming the transcript into various exercises for the class is as well. Cloze exercises, sentence scrambling, even deleted lines in dialogs to be completed are all motivating student-generated activities.

Activity D. Visual analysis

Visual conventions are many times universal. Have learners locate a television commercial from the target culture. Provide basic descriptive terminology that they may need to present an in-depth analysis of the visual aspects of the commercial. Have learners present, share and discuss one another's analyses basing this in any new understanding of the target culture they may have gleaned.

Activity E. Evaluating the learning

Tracking learner progress can be greatly facilitated via written synchronous environments. Indeed, a complete running record of learner language development can be maintained using archives of the synchronous sessions along with submitted assignments. These records can be shared with and/or assembled by the student in an electronic portfolio, an excellent evaluation device for language education. What other items might appear in students' e-portfolios? Develop rubrics (Chapter 2) for students to self assess.

References

Blake, R. (2000) Computer-mediated communication: A window on L2 Spanish interlanguage. *Language Learning & Technology* 4 (1), 120–136.

Doughty, C. and Long, M. (2003) Optimal psycholinguistic environments for distance foreign language learning. *Language Learning & Technology* 7 (3), 50–80.

Ene, E., Görtler, S. and McBride, K. (2005) Teacher participation styles in foreign language chats and their effects on student behavior. *The Computer Assisted Language Instruction Consortium Journal* 22 (3), 603–634.

Jones, R. (2004) The problem of context in computer mediated communication. In P. Levine and R. Scollon (eds) *Discourse & technology multimodal discourse analysis* (pp. 20–33). Washington DC: Georgetown University Press.

Lai, C. and Zhao, Y. (2006) Noticing and text-based chat. *Language Learning & Technology* 10 (3), 102–120.

Lluna-Mateu, F. R. (2006) Development of Spanish l2 competence in a synchronous CMC (chat room) environment: The role of visually-enhanced recasts in fostering grammatical knowledge and changes in communicative language use. Unpublished doctoral dissertation, Louisiana State University.

Meskill, C. and Anthony, N. (2005) Foreign language learning with CMC: Forms of online instructional discourse in a hybrid Russian class. *System* 33 (1), 89–105

Pellettieri, J. (2000) Negotiation in cyberspace: The role of chatting in the development of grammatical competence. In M. Warschauer and R. Kerns (eds) *Network-based language teaching: Concepts and practice* (pp. 59–86). Cambridge: Cambridge University Press.

Smith, B. (2003) The use of communication strategies in computer-mediated communication. *System* 31, 29–53.

Smith, B. (2004) Computer-mediated negotiated interaction and lexical acquisition. *Studies in Second Language Acquisition* 26, 365–398.

Sotillo, S. M. (2000) Discourse functions and syntactic complexity in synchronous and asynchronous communication. *Language Learning & Technology*, 4 (1), 82–119.

6

Language learning and teaching in written asynchronous environments

- The characteristics and affordances that make written asynchronous environments useful for language education are presented and discussed.

- Detailed illustrations and their contexts provide a sense of how and why instructional conversations best work in these environments.

- Variations on pedagogical uses for written asynchronous environments are included.

Language learning and teaching in written asynchronous environments

Objectives

In this chapter you will learn:

- the definition of written asynchronous environments;
- the special affordances of written asynchronous environments;
- how different instructional conversation strategies can be undertaken in these environments;
- how the environment's affordances can be taken advantage of to support and amplify these conversations.

Overview

Written asynchronous online learning environments are the most popular and the most widely used of the four. While it is the most technologically simple, accessible and mechanically easy to use, it nonetheless, like the other three environments, requires a great deal of reconceptualization regarding teaching and learning processes. Both commercial and non-commercial written asynchronous utilities have been around in various forms for as long as there have been publicly accessible telecommunications. As early as the late 1980s, instructors used written asynchronous in various ways to post course materials, conduct learning activities, share learner assignments and communicate with learners between live meetings. In some cases, online activities became the equivalent of actual seat time in the f2f classroom, a practice that came to be known as *blended learning*. In the mid-1990s, online written asynchronous utilities became sufficiently sophisticated that instructors began to migrate their entire courses into written asynchronous formats. When this migration was done expertly with the design of the online instruction exploiting the features and affordances that maximized the online instructional experience, both instructors and students came to enjoy and often prefer online to live meetings. The flexibility in terms of time and place, along with a strong sense of a learning community, compounded with the fact that participation structures allowed for all students to exercise equal voice continue to make online learning an attractive option.

Because written asynchronous environments have been around the longest and have been used the most widely, the bulk of research undertaken on online learning has focused on how teaching and learning unfold in this environment. In language education particularly, analysis of learners' written asynchronous utterances has been a popular topic of research. In our own work, we have found that the most important element in successful online language learning is teacher-orchestrated instructional conversations. In the following sections, we again discuss each of the online instructional conversation strategies in turn with examples of how these unfold in written asynchronous environments, a venue where instructors and students enjoy the luxury of time to fully engage teachable moments.

There are some caveats, however, based on many years of experience with teaching in written asynchronous venues. When a language task is assigned in written asynchronous environments, time can work both for and against its productive accomplishment. Because fully online asynchronous courses have flexible participation structures, agreements concerning how often students are to log in and participate are critical. As part of any set of instructions for pair or group or whole class work, a clear indication must be made about participation expectations. Pair dynamics will not have a chance if only one member of the pair logs on. Likewise with small groups. In a group of three, if one member fails to log on within a defined period of time, the other members will feel shortchanged. Thus, stating log on requirements and reinforcing these are critical to maintaining an equitable, felicitous community of learners.

Calling attention to forms

In written asynchronous environments, calling attention to forms and particular lexical items can be done quite readily via a number of techniques. Again, the element of time allows for careful, thoughtful responses on the part of instructors to the teachable moments that present themselves in asynchronous conversations. Not only can instructors make use of the visual strategies for calling attention that have been discussed in the previous chapters (using capital letters, color, font, size, animations, circling, underlining, etc.), but also inserted and linked to images, video clips, audio clips, reference material and the like. Internal links to other relevant posts within the course are also possible; e.g. remember when we focused on X? (*link to prior course conversation*). This internal linking nicely builds an internal coherence to a language course by reminding learners of the whole and the parts of their learning experiences.

A written asynchronous language class can develop its own conventions for signaling attention to aspects of the target language. Indeed, learners can take on responsibility for using the group-established conventions themselves by signaling attention to one another in threaded discussions during task-based activities. These conventions can be developed as the course progresses – a special area is set up for conventions to be suggested, discussed and determined – or at the start of the course as an introductory unit – how will we signal what should be attended to as we converse in this environment? In either case, active instructional participation on the part of all learners can only serve to enrich the learning experience for all.

Task-level attention to form

As with the other three learning environments, the design and continual use of the **task toolkit** is an essential aspect of teaching in written asynchronous environments. In addition to their central role in delineating focal language for a given task, these can be archived and referred to throughout the course as well as used by individual and groups of students for unit reviews.

For the following task, mid-beginning learners of EFL are instructed to read a simplified top news story of the day, summarize it and state an opinion. The **task toolkit** contains key language for summarizing and expressing an opinion in English. This information is continuously visible on the screen as learners compose their posts, read one another's posts and respond to one another's posts.

Summarizing
In brief,
In sum,
The main event/idea is

Expressing an Opinion
In my opinion,
To my way of thinking,
I think that
I believe that

When either the instructor or other students detect a need for one or more of these language elements in a learner's post, they can use the task-level attention to form instructional conversation move by explicitly pointing this out, inserting a commonly understood symbol that indicates the poster should refer to the **task toolkit**, or more implicitly guide the poster to rephrase using the key language elements of the task.

Incidental attention to forms

Attention can be drawn to any aspect of learner output that the instructor tracks as having been studied and therefore used correctly while the class is engaged in any activity, not just one targeting that form or lexical item. In the following, an intermediate EFL class is having a general discussion of a movie they had all viewed independently. The instructor responds to this teachable moment:

S: I think he should get all the money. His work is what made the money!
T: So, you think he **should have gotten** (*link to modal perfect task toolkit*) all the money? What about you others? **Should he have gotten** all the money?

In this way she draws attention to a form that the class had studied two weeks earlier in a way that furthers the content and spirit of the conversation.

Time and media affordances allow teachers to make incidental attention to form more salient. In the fast paced f2f classroom, teachers often do not have opportunities to call attention to forms incidentally arising in a conversation. In written asynchronous environments, teachers can underline the targeted forms by using links and references to grammar notes and **task toolkits**. In the example from an intermediate Russian II course, the instructor responds to a student's utterance by inserting a link to a grammar note right under the word in which the student made a grammatical mistake. She also embeds into her post a **task toolkit** from a previous lesson.

S: мой русский друг говорит, что южанин из Америки слишком много приветливы. Мы всегду улыбаемся, говорим и махаем рукой каждому. Он думает что мы едим странную пищу... Гритс, вареный арахис и чай со льдом. Он также думает, что мы двигаемся медленно. Он хотит спешить! [My Russian friend says that a Southern from America is too friendly. We always smile, talk and wave with a hand to everyone. He thinks that we eat strange food... Grits, boiled peanuts and iced tea. He also thinks that we move slowly. He wants (*incorrect form*) to rush!]

T: Если он хочет всегда спешить, то ему лучше жить в Москве. В Москве все спешат. Там очень быстрый ритм жизни. [If he wants (*correct verb under which there is a link to the grammar note in a previous lesson*) to always rush, it's better for him to live in Moscow. In Moscow everybody is in a rush. There is a fast life rhythm. (*embedded image of a grammar note as in Figure 100*)

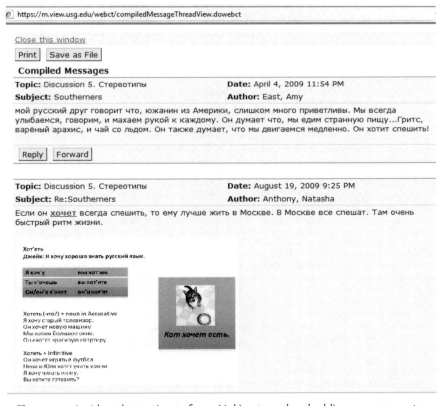

Figure 100 Incidental attention to form. Linking to and embedding grammar notes

Calling attention to lexis

As we have seen, attention to particular vocabulary items can be drawn by any number of visual, auditory and multimodal means. The affordance of asynchronous instruction, of course, is that as much time as need be taken can be used productively by both instructor and students to mark or annotate lexical items that occur in threaded discussions. It is through the visual and aural amplification of new or recycled words in the target language in multiple and novel contexts that mastery of these items is attained. Their multimodal attributes serve to make these words more comprehensible and memorable.

Task-level attention to lexis

Caches of recycled lexical items can be stored and accessed in any number of ways and students can be encouraged to use these in their own instructional conversation strategies as a way to review for tests or as a means of preparing and composing posts for a given language learning task. This sample class of mid-beginning learners of Spanish has been brainstorming and assembling semantic nets for different kinds of foods one might find at themed restaurants. They have generated the following semantic net for seafood items in a seafood restaurant (Figure 101).

Scents, tastes, ways of preparing			
	Smells	Tastes	Ways of Preparing
peces espadas (swordfish)	huele a pescado (fishy smell)	fuerte (strong)	hervido (boiled)
camarón (shrimp)	el olor del mar (smell of the sea)	dulce (sweet)	frito (fried)
platija (flounder)	un olor fuerte (a strong smell)	parecido a la goma (rubbery)	cocido al vapor (steamed)
langosta (lobster)	un olor dulce (a sweet smell)		cocido al horno (baked)
conchas de peregrino (scallops)			

Figure 101 Task toolkit for lexical collocations

In groups of four, their task is to develop a script for two couples eating in such a restaurant that includes an ordering sequence and small talk/critique about the food that is served. These scripts are collaboratively composed by the groups, then posted for the rest of the class. They are encouraged to include illustrations (links and/or pasted in images, audio or video files) to accompany the scenes they present (Figure 102). When Group A posts their script to the class, the instructor notices that two of the four group members ordered and commented on the same seafood dish. She interjects, calling attention to new lexical items that might be used in their stead.

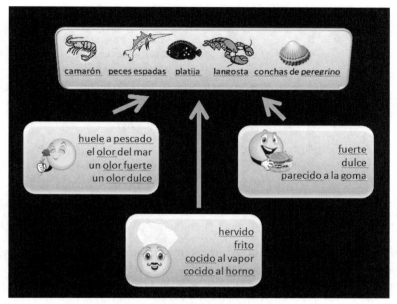

Figure 102 Task-level attention to lexis. Semantic net

T: Muy bien pero vos dos comen las mismas platas. Porqué no come otra clase de pescados? Langosta, platija ... [Good, but you both had the same dish. Why don't you try some other kind of fish? Lobster? Flounder?]

Here she also inserts a picture of each of her suggestions into the post to tempt the group members (Figure 103).

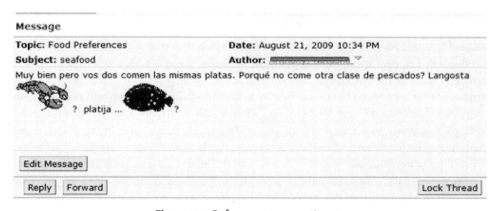

Figure 103 Reference to semantic net

In an online elementary Russian II class, the instructor uses a vocabulary-focused activity as the **task toolkit**. From the four images provided in the activity, students who know the words белый [white] and черный [black] are to figure out the meanings of the adjectives короткий [short], длинный [long], узкий [tights] and широкий [loose]. A screenshot is displayed in the instructor's initial post on the discussion topic *What Clothes are Appropriate to Wear to What Places?* In her description of the task and models, the instructor refers to the **task toolkit** via arrows (Figure 104).

Figure 104 Task-level attention to lexis

With the help of arrows, the instructor signals students to use the target adjectives.

T: (*task description*) Что можно носить на работу? В университет? На дискотеку? Дома? Можно носить на работу короткие узкие платья? Можно носить дома широкую удобную одежду? Можно носить в университет длинные широкие шорты? [What is appropriate to wear to work? To college? To a disco club? At home? Is it appropriate to wear short tight dresses to work? Is it appropriate to wear loose comfortable clothes at home? Is it appropriate to wear long loose shorts to a college?]

S: На работу я обычно ношу юбку и блузку и туфли. [I usually wear a skirt and a blouse and shoes to work.]

T: Узкую →||← юбку или широкую ←| |→ юбку? [Tight →||← skirt or a loose ←| |→ skirt?]

Incidental attention to Lexis

Because learners have all the time they need to seek out the target language vocabulary that they need in composing their asynchronous posts, there is a higher likelihood of misuse or odd use of lexical items. As we well know, looking up translations and equivalents can often lead to odd collocations. This tendency to look up and use new words can present numerous teachable moments whereby the instructor and/or classmates highlight and provide commentary and remediation on incorrect uses of target language vocabulary. The availability of free concordancing tools whereby vast corpora of written and spoken target language can be accessed and the lexical item in question be run in order to assess successful collocations makes these teachable moments of calling attention to lexis easily managed. Indeed, simply highlighting a learner's misuse of a vocabulary word and asking 'Did you run this?' (use the concordance program) may constitute a response that suffices in pointing the learner to the need for more independent research on the word in question.

In the following example, advanced learners of ESL have been assigned to annotate or 'illuminate' a poem. Annotations or illuminations can take the form of learner-generated text, audio video or animations that they embed within the poem for others to access.

T: It's bleak the night
When the sun's at rest
The day's events
Sorry remnants still.
Fragile skin and eyes now
Saved from the burn,
The bright. ----

In one of the annotations a pair of learners writes the following:

Ss: The poem's narrator implies here that his skin cannot cope with more sun and heat.

The instructor, noting that the term 'cope with' is misused as the line of the poem indicates that the narrator's skin cannot tolerate the heat, posts the students' sentence with the words 'cope with' highlighted. She adds the following lexical heuristic and encourages the pair to run both 'cope with' and 'tolerate' through the concordance program to see with what words each collocates.

T: skin=inanimate, 'cope with' implies volition and purpose

Run 'cope with' (*link inserted*) and 'tolerate' (*link inserted*) and report back the words with which each collocates. (Figure 105)

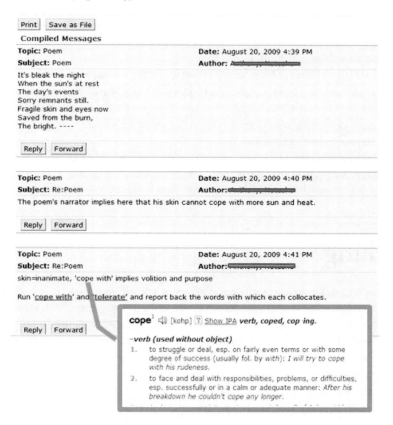

Figure 105 Incidental attention to lexis

In an additional example, an intermediate Russian instructor begins the following discussion:

T: For these two weeks you will participate in the discussion forum on the topic "Идеальная работа" [Ideal Job]. Provide 4 features of your ideal job. As a class you will discuss those features and reach agreement on what feature (ONE) is the most important. Provide all pros and cons. During these two weeks, you will have to post at least three messages to this discussion board.

Students use dictionaries for this assignment which can present word choice problems. When one of the students uses an incorrect word, the instructor continues the discussion using a more appropriate word, demonstrating its natural use in a conversation on the topic.

S: Когда как (хорошая медицинская и зубная страховки, и гибкий график работы), я согласен. Но, я хочу работа что интерересная и другая. Во-первых, Интересная работа будет ***просыпаться***. Во-вторых, хочу работаю в изменение окружение-- не хочу врач кто лечит болных ежедневно. С другой стороны я хочу работать за рубежом или где можно путешествовать часто. Хочу работать в министерство иностранных деле так как я хочу работа что интересная, другая, и можно путешествовать много раз. [When there is a good medical and dental insurance and flexible work schedule, I agree. But I want the job to be interesting and different. First of all, an interesting job ***will wake up***. Second, I want to work in a changing environment. I don't want to be a doctor who cures patients every day. On the other hand, I want a job abroad or where I can travel often. I want to work for a Ministry of Foreign Affairs as I want a job that is interesting, different and allowing for often traveling.]

T: Согласна! Интересная работа, которая ***держит*** нас ***в тонусе***, когда каждый день что-то новое, это здорово. С другой стороны, когда каждый день всё новое, это значит, много стресса. Нет? [I agree. Interesting job that ***keeps*** us ***awake***, when every day brings something new is great. On the other hand, when every day everything is new it means a lot of stress. No?]

S: Да, когда каждый день всё новое, значит много стресса. Но, это очень интересный:) [Yes, when every day everything is new, it means a lot of stress. But it is very interesting :)]

Corralling

As we have seen in oral asynchronous environments, corralling is especially well facilitated by the element of time: time for students to compose their posts, time for instructors to detect and design corralling strategies in response to teachable moments and time for all to consider and reflect on instructional conversations overall. Corralling is an effective instructional strategy for getting learners back on track attending to and employing the targeted language of the moment in ways that assist them in incorporating that language into their developing repertoire. As we have discussed, employing this kind of redirecting strategy as part of the natural stream of communication is an effective method for teaching learners to notice, attend to, comprehend and use new language productively.

Task-level corralling

An example of corralling is in a mid-beginning EFL class. The class is taught entirely in written asynchronous mode and learners have been assigned the roles as 'fast food coordinators'. Their job, in groups of four, is to develop a schedule for the preparation of food at a fast food restaurant. The **task toolkit** contains the focal language, some of which is new to students (time intervals and measurement) and some of which is being recycled from an earlier activity (food preparation vocabulary) (Figures 106 and 107).

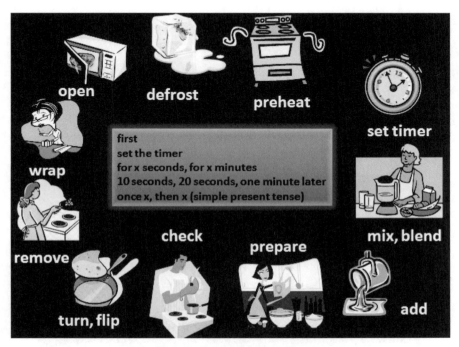

Figure 106 Task-level coralling

open	first
defrost	set the timer
preheat	for x seconds, for x minutes
timer	10 seconds, 20 seconds, one minute later
mix, blend	once x, then x (simple present tense)
add	
prepare	
check	
turn, flip	
remove	
wrap	

Figure 107 Task Toolkit

Over a week, the four groups work on the written schedules that they will share with the whole class. While monitoring their task-based discussions, their instructor notices that learners are tending to avoid using the time expressions listed in the **task toolkit** by simply listing the actions. She uses a corralling strategy within the following group conversation:

S1: Okay. We start with defrost meat.
S2: Okay. Open meat package.
S3: Defrost the bread also.
S4: And defrost french fries.
T: Guys, use this: first, x, then, once x, then x. Okay?
S4: First defrost meat.
T: First defrost the meat for....?
S3: First defrost the meat for three hours.
T: Bravo. And then?

In the next example, a high beginning ESL teacher assigns the task of accounting for a recommendation (should) by using a comparative construction (Figure 108)

S1: I think he should go out with Linda because she practices yoga.
T: So, you think Linda is more _____ than Carla?
S1: Right. Linda is more fit than Carla.

Figure 108 Task-level corralling

Incidental corralling

Based on any prior task focus, corralling can be employed throughout the written asynchronous course or course component as a form of recycling and review of new language. Even if learners are not using this language, if the context of situation calls for something that they have already explicitly studied, then corralling learners into attending to and possibly producing the known language can be developmentally powerful. It is, essentially, reminding learners of what they already know in a communicative context.

In the following example, low intermediate learners of French have been asked to recount their weekend activities – a regular feature of this fully online written asynchronous course for native speakers of English. Weeks earlier the class had encountered one of many of the faux amis (false friends, false cognates that typically trip up English speakers). In one of the student's accounts, they misuse the French *finalment* meaning *eventually* in English, not finally.

S1: Et puis, apres tout ça, je suis rentré chez moi finalment. [And so, after all I came home eventually.]

T: Ça veux dire vous êtes rentré chez vous....? (rappelez-vous les faux amis) [Do you mean to say the you came home...? (remember the false friends/cognates)]

S1: Pardon. Je suis rentré chez moi enfin. [Sorry. I came home finally.]

T: Et voila. C'etait bien passé enfin le weekend? [There you go. Was your weekend enjoyable after all?]

S1: Oui. Enfin c'etait bien passé. [Yes. After all it was enjoyable.]

In the next example, intermediate Russian learners are discussing the topic of 'Natural Disasters' The instructor seizes the opportunity to direct a student who is writing in English to express his ideas in Russian with the use of constructions he already knows. The instructor corrals the student into using his passive knowledge in active communication in a real-life situation.

S1: На 29 августе 2005 году ураган Катрина прошёл через Ню Орлеанс. Ветер разрушил здания и сломал деревья. Электричество, воды, канализации не было. Многие люди, которые не уезжали из города, поднимались на крыши и ждали спасения. Сразу после урагана банды грабили магазины и квартиры. [On August 29, 2005 the hurricane Katrina went through New Orleans. The wind demolished buildings and broke trees. There was not any electricity, water, and sewer. Many people who did not leave the city mounted the roofs and waited to be rescued. Immediately after the hurricane gangs robbed the stores and apartments.]

S2: I hate you! Just Kidding. I was writing about Katrina as well.

T: Надо писать по-русски: Я тебя ненавижу! :))))))))))) Хотя это слишком сильно будет для русского языка. Русские обычно так не шутят. Они могут сказать "Как ты могла?" - что-то такое. [You have to write in Russian: I hate you! :)))))))))) Although it is too strong for the Russian language. Russians usually do not joke like that. They can say "How could you?" – something like that.]

S2: Джекки как ты могла? ;) на теме: Грустно видеть как ураган превращает невинные народы во банды :([Jackie how could you? ;) on topic: It is sad to see how the hurricane turns innocent people into gangs.]

Saturating

As we have pointed out in the other three online environments, the more often learners encounter elements of the target language in meaningful contexts, the more likely they are to incorporate these into their developing target language repertoires. In written asynchronous formats, saturating posts with target language elements under study can be as natural as it is in the live classroom. Instructors and students can both make a point of using targeted forms and lexical items repeatedly as they converse to reinforce the learning. And, of course, targets can be highlighted and annotated in a variety of ways to further draw learner attention to them. In the following example of beginning learners of EFL, the instructor uses a focal vocabulary word *name* as frequently as possible while encouraging the learners in her fully online written asynchronous class to do the same.

T: My **name** is Molly. That is my **name**. Please call me by that **name**. I want to know your **names** also. Mohamed. Is that your **name?**
S1:   Yes. Mohamed.
T: Your **name** is Mohamed?
S1:   Yes my name is Mohamed.

In this next example, an instructor starts the topic 'Getting Advice: From Mom or Dad?' He saturates his topic explanation with the construction 'who would you' using it with different verbs, which helps learners focus on and in turn use the construction.

T: When you have a problem in life, *who would you turn to* first: your mom or dad? Of course, friends are important in making decisions, but if you had to choose between your mom or dad for help, *who would you ask?* Does it depend on the situation and topic? If so, share your experiences and feelings about this topic. For example, *who would you talk to* first in this case: You need advice about breaking up with a girlfriend or boyfriend. If for whatever reason you can't ask a parent, *who would you turn to* for advice?

Using linguistic traps

Written asynchronous environments might be considered the best of the four for the successful use of linguistic traps. Again, the element of time to 'set the trap' and for learners to compose and post a 'trapped' response makes a large difference as does the fact that the conversation is written and can therefore be referenced any number of times. As we have seen, linguistic traps can be set with words, the instructor's or students', and, as in the following example, they can also be set using visuals.

In this high intermediate academic ESL class, students are working on their skills at composing academic papers for their future undergraduate courses. They are currently working on developing a comparison and contrast essay. In preparation, they have researched a topic of their choice to compare and contrast and have read and discussed a number of sample essays. They will post at least three drafts of their essays to the entire class for feedback. As they develop their drafts, the following **task toolkit** is present in the area of the course where they post and comment on each others' work (Figure 109).

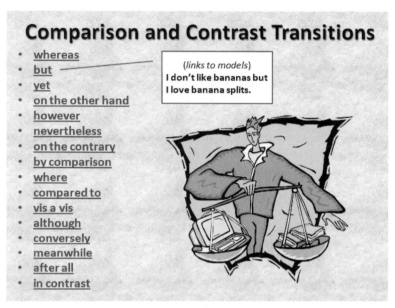

Figure 109 Using linguistic traps

A student's preliminary draft could benefit from using such comparison and contrast transitions. A classmate detects this and traps his online colleague into incorporating transitions in his subsequent draft:

S1: Nice job on this first draft. In your third and fourth sentence you say *The outdoor markets in Turkey are nosier than those in the U.S. The markets in the U.S. have more diverse products than those in Turkey.* Combine the two sentences using one of the transition words in the *task toolkit*. That will make reading this smoother because the writing will be more connected.

In the following, a Russian instructor in an elementary Russian II class asks questions so as to trap students into using prepositional case endings in describing locations and places to work.

T: Ты хочешь работать *в полиции*? [Do you want to work *at the police*?]
S1: Я хочу работать *в лаборатории*. [I want to work *at the lab*.]
T: Я живу *в штате* Нью-Йорк, но я хочу жить *в Мэриленде*. Там тепло и нет снега. Там океан. [I live *in* New York *state* but I want to live *in Maryland*. There is warm and no snow. There is an ocean.]
S2: Я тоже хочу жить где тепло и много сонце. [I also want to live where it's warm and a lot of sun.]
T: Где? *Во Флориде*? Или *в Калифорнии*? [Where? *In Florida*? Or *in California*?]
S2: *Во Флориде.* [**In Florida**.]

T: А почему не **в Калифорнии**? Там же тоже много солнца и тепло. Но я не знаю, там океан холодный или тёплый? [Why not **in California**? There is also a lot of sun and warm. But I don't know if the ocean there is cold or warm.]

S2:   Да, **в Калифорнии** океан холодный. [Yes, the ocean is cold **in California**.]

Modeling

Modeling new language in written asynchronous environments does not have to be confined to text only. Incorporating sound, image and video files that model the target language elements is always possible and, when it comes to emphasizing pronunciation, intonation and listening practice, it is essential.

In written asynchronous environments, modeling can be as simple as providing a conversational opener. In this example, an intermediate EFL instructor has posted a series of pictures of various people in the process of undertaking tasks. He models the target structure – the present perfect tense, and learners follow his lead.

T: What has he been doing? He has been painting his kitchen. What an ugly color! Ugh! What has she been doing?

S: She has been walking her dog. What an ugly dog! Mine so much pretier :)

Models can be easily picked up by students due to the written nature of this online communication venue. In this example, a Russian instructor models the construction 'to be/to become + Instrumental case' for a student unfamiliar with the construction. The student not only picks up the modeled structure but also uses it with a different word.

S: Я хочу учусь на факультете криминологии. Это очень хорошо в университете Торонто. [I want to major in criminology. It's good at the University of Toronto.]

T: Вы хотите **быть юристом**? [To you want **to be a lawyer**?]

S: Я хочу **быть криминалистом**. Это очень интересно. [I want **to be a criminologist**. It is very interesting.]

Further, models are often provided in descriptions of tasks as in the following Russian example.

T: During the following two weeks, you will participate in a discussion on the topic "Your family." You have to post at least two messages asking your classmates one question about their families and answering other people's questions. You can ask any questions related to the family: Какая твоя семья? Кто твоя мама? Как её зовут? Кто твой папа? Как его зовут? [What kind is your family? Who is your Mom? What is her name? Who is your Dad? What is his name?]

S1:   Здраствуйте. Моя семья маленькая. У меня есть мама, папа, и брат. Какая ваша семья? [Hello. My family is small. I have Mom, Dad, and a brother. What kind is your family?]

S2:   Кто твой брат? Как его зовут? [What is your brother? What is his name?]

S1:   Мои брат школьник. Он зовут карлос. Кто твоя сестра? Как ее зовут? [My brother is a school student. His name is Carlos. Who is your sister? What is her name?]

For the discussion 'Come sono loro?' an Italian instructor models possible constructions and vocabulary.

T: **Modelo: [model]**
        Io parlo di Dario Fo: Lui è un uomo molto simpatico e molto intelligente. Lui ha una personalità molto divertente e creativa.
        Lui è dinamico e molto diretto.
        Dario Fo è vecchio. Lui ha gli occhi azzurri. Lui ha i capelli bianchi, e lui è un poco calvo.
        Dario Fo è molto contento. [I speak about Dario Fo: He is a very likeable and intelligent man. He has a very funny and creative personality. He is dynamic and multidimensional. Dario Fo is old. He has blue eyes. He has grey hair, and he is a little bald. Dario Fo is content.]

S1:   Io parlo di Silvio Berlusconi:
        Lui e bello e ricco italiano. Silvio ha i capelli castano e gli occhi marrone. Lui e faccia bello. Lui e molto fortunato essere famoso. [I speak about Silvio Berlusconi: He is a handsome and rich Italian. Silvio has brown hair and brown eyes. This makes him handsome. He is very lucky to be famous.]

S2:   Caio John
        Io parlo Silvio Berlussconi anche. Lui e molto interessente. [Hi John. I speak about Silvio Berlusconi as well. He is very interesting.]

S3:   Silvio sguardo molto ricco. Si? [Is Silvio very rich? Really?]

S4:   Ciao John! Molto Bene descrizione. Siamo Simile. [Hello John! Very good description. We think similarly.]

Providing explicit feedback

In the live classroom when instructors provide explicit feedback, several things can happen. Students may not attend to it, students may attend to it but not incorporate it in amended output, only some learners will attend, the student(s) to whom the explicit feedback is directed will clam up from embarrassment and the explicit feedback may be misconstrued and its intended effect thus lost as activities progress. In written asynchronous environments, however, the feedback does not disappear and cannot be ignored, learners to whom it is addressed have time to consider the feedback and revise accordingly, and less outgoing students who might not be as responsive in a live situation are empowered by both time and 'face' issues to react positively.

Just as in the other environments, explicit feedback can be as straightforward as pointing the learner to the **task toolkit** if one of the rules there has been violated, inserting a symbol that represents a rule or concept, or simply stating what needs to be corrected outright. In this example of explicit feedback in a blended low level Spanish course that meets one-third of the time in a written asynchronous course space, intermediate learners are carrying out a collaborative shopping task whereby groups of four are examining and comparing the value of items in online stores. The language focus is on making comparisons and expressing preferences (Figure 110).

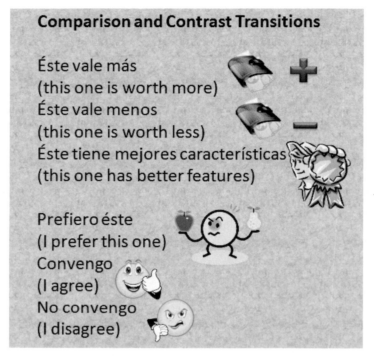

Figure 110 Providing explicit feedback

S1: Me gusto esto (*link to product description*) [I like that one]
S2: Prefiero este (*link to different product description*) [I like this one]
S1: No convengo. Este mejor. [I don't. This better.]
T: Decimos **Éste tiene mejores características.** [We say this one has better features.]

In this example, students from a Japanese university learning English created blogs as a part of their ESL courses. They were assigned to introduce their favorite parts of the Japanese culture. Their instructor encouraged English speakers to comment on students' blogs: 'Please keep all comments civil and in English. Corrections are welcome and much appreciated!'

NNS: Anytime I am in my house, I listen the music or watch TV. So I introduce my favorite singer, "Chara", and my favorite drama series, "働きマン".
NS: My favorite band in Japan right now is Uverworld. I will look up your favorite singer later tonight! Your English is fine...however, you said in the beginning "Anytime I am in my house, I listen the music or watch TV" I would say, "Whenever I am in my house, I listen to music or watch TV." This sounds a little more natural!

Providing implicit feedback

What are the implications and affordances of delayed time and text as mediums for implicit feedback? Signals to learners for needed amendments to their output can, like in synchronous and live environments be as subtle as raised eyebrows ^^ or as unsubtle as 'Try again'. Because these signals are in text form and time independent, learners can attend to them more carefully with the aid of any number of resources to use in changing their text utterance to the correct form while the informational or content dimension of the utterance remains intact. As has been illustrated throughout the other three environments, signaling implicitly can take the form of sounds, symbols, links, inserted recordings and, of course, simple text.

In the following example, mid-beginning learners of EFL are discussing the places that they would like to visit in the US. The **task toolkit** contains the rules for using the definite article *the* with place names. It also contains the symbol ↓ to indicate the need for the definite article with place names.

S1:   I want to visit Empire State Building, Niagara Falls, and Grand Canyon.

The instructor cuts, pastes and inserts implicit feedback.

T: So, you want to visit ↓ Empire State Building, Niagara Falls, and ↓ Grand Canyon? Do you want to visit other places as well?

S1:   Yes, with the Empire State Building, Niagara Falls, and the Grand Canyon, I want to visit Hollywood!

In comments to an ESL blog, one of the students posted a comment with an error. Another participant gently corrected him by providing the correct form in his own utterance that was a part of a meaningful conversation about a trip to Disneyland.

P1:   I'm also going to go Disneyland on next Wednesday! I'm looking forward to go. *Let's talking* about Disneyland in April!!

P2:   That is such a great thing that you are going to Disneyland. Yes! *Let's talk* about your trip in April when you get back. (Figure 111)

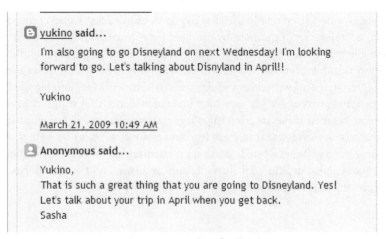

Figure 111 Implicit feedback

In an elementary Russian II class, an instructor corrects her student's incorrect use of the Instrumental case during the discussion about students' future professions. In the same class, students discuss their daily routines. Two students use the verb 'to go' in its incorrect form, unidirectional instead of multidirectional. The instructor intervenes with an implicit correction, using this verb in her utterance, which is meaningfully connected to the previous conversation.

S: Я хочу быть **астронавта**. Они работают в Хьюстон в штате Техасе. [I want to be an **astronaut** (*incorrect ending*). They work in Huston in the state of Texas.]

T: Ты хочешь быть **астронавтом**? Ты хочешь летать на Луну? [Do you want to be an **astronaut** (*correct ending*)? Do you want to go to the Moon?]

S: Да, я очень хочу быть **астронавтом**. Я очень много хочу летать на Луну и Марс тоже! [Yes, I want to be an **astronaut** (*correct ending*) very much. I want very much to go to the Moon and Mars too!]

S1:   Мне нравится делать что-нибудь новое каждый день. [I like to do something new every day.]

S2:   Вам не нравится каждый день идти в класс? [You don't like **to go** (*wrong verb*) to class every day?]

S1:   Нет, я не хочу идти в класс каждый день. [Yes, I don't want **to go** (*wrong verb*) to class every day.]

T: Я тоже не хочу ходить в класс каждый день. Поэтому я преподаю онлайн :))))))) [I also don't want **to go** (*right verb*) to class every day. That's why I teach online :))))))]

S3:   Мне нравится ходить в клас но не каждый день. [I like **to go** (*right verb*) to class but not every day.]

Summary

As we pointed out at the start of this chapter, written asynchronous environments are at present the most widely used due to the ease of accessibility of text-based communication tools and to the irrelevance of moment-by-moment time. Such affordances mean a wide range of possible practices, practices that do not need to be limited to text, but that can incorporate any number of multimodal features to amplify the learning. After nearly two decades of widening use of written asynchronous environments for both blended and fully online instructional purposes, we have a solid body of evidence that supports positive learning outcomes when these are used in pedagogically sound ways. For language education, there is also evidence that these learning forums can work as well, if not better, than f2f environments when talented educators recognize and in turn exploit their key affordances: spoken text, multimodal amplification, archives, and the time to read, reference, consider and compose.

End of chapter activities

Activity A. Designing an activity for written asynchronous instruction

Design an activity (task toolkit, topic, questions, models, examples, etc.) for a text-based discussion in the language you teach. Working in pairs, present your activity to your partner. Discuss in what ways designing the activity the way you did is more beneficial for language learners than merely providing them with a topic for a text-based discussion.

Activity B. Comparing two types of discussions

During one week, participate in two different discussion topics (in groups of five to six participants if your class is too large), posting at least three messages to each:

1. *An ideal student*: What qualities should an ideal student have, the one you would always like to have in your class? As a group, identify three of the most important features of an ideal student. Negotiate and compromise. Your final group product is the list of three most important qualities of an ideal student.

2. *Good and bad experiences*: What good and bad experiences did you have working with students?

During your next class meeting, discuss the participation, linguistic production, logistical outcome and other features of these two discussion threads. What have you observed? What makes a discussion more productive and why?

Activity C. Working with an excerpt

Read the following excerpt from an ESL class discussion. What have you observed? What instructional moves have you identified in this piece? How would you have handled this student's post?

S: One phrase from that movie is "I think that's not that **big a deal**." The structure seems a little strange, isn't it. I only know people would say "I think that is not a big deal."

T: The way you have written "not that big a deal" **does** seem strange, **doesn't** it? You have written it the way you heard it. The correct form is "that's not that big of a deal". It is an idiom that means *it's not very important.*

Activity D. Providing your own examples

For at least three out of eight instructional moves identified in this chapter, find your own examples from the classes you teach. If you do not currently teach any classes, go to online discussion forums for learners of the language you teach and observe those exchanges. Participate in such discussions as a language expert, using instructional moves you have learned in this chapter. Working in small groups, report your examples and findings to your group.

Activity E. Generating meaningful and form-focused discussion postings

Look at the following discussion posting. Working for 10 minutes in pairs or small groups of three to four, generate the best answer to this posting. Consider the affordances and pitfalls of the written asynchronous medium.

S: Hi. I'm japanese student ☺ I'm going to spesk about marriage. Do you want to marrage or not? In my case, I don't want to marriage.becouse my dream is singer. Now I have many audition for singer but my results is bad ☹ I don't want to make many sacrifices to become a singer. It is most important for me to challenge my dream. If my dreams come true, I will be able to satisfaction my life and think about marriage again. Plesae tell me your dream.

Activity F. Blogging

Blogs can be considered as written asynchronous environments. However, the nature of blogs is distinct in that posters usually add provocative comments that are rarely related to the comments of others. Blog participants concentrate not on engaging and sustaining meaningful interaction, but rather on expressing their personal opinions. Nonetheless, blogs can still be used in language instruction to great effect by capitalizing on this opinion-oriented aspect. Have a look at several blogs (e.g. http://blogspot.com) and consider how you might offer language assistance to posters via instructional conversations.

Further reading

O'Rourke, B. (2005) Form-focused interaction in online tandem learning. *The Computer Assisted Language Instruction Consortium Journal* 22 (3), 433–66.

Savignon, S. and Roithmeier, W. (2004) Computer-mediated communication: Texts and strategies. *The Computer Assisted Language Instruction Consortium Journal* 21 (2), 265–290.

Simpson, J. (2005) Conversational floors in synchronous text-based CMC discourse. *Discourse Studies* 7 (3), 337–361.

Weasenforth, D., Biesenbach-Lucas, S. and Meloni, C. (2002) Realizing constructivist objectives through collaborative technologies: Threaded discussions. *Language Learning of Technology* 6 (3), 58–86.

7

Written venues amplified via sound and visuals

This chapter summarizes the written venues discussed in Chapters 5 and 6 and expands the notion of amplifying written instruction using sound and visuals. The following amplifications are discussed and illustrated:

- Non-intrusiveness

- Time savers and gatekeepers

- Salience

- Accessibility

- Familiarity

Written venues amplified via sound and visuals

Online instructional conversations in written venues can be amplified in two ways:

- **Aural** communication can be used with text being a primary means of communication. Aural components can be incorporated to complement the textual component.

- Written communication can be made highly **visualized** using images, symbols, emoticons, charts, fonts, videos, sound files, links to audios and videos, embedded visuals, etc.

Five factors are in play in the evolution of written communication venues for language education:

1. Sound and visuals incorporated into written venues render interruptions in the form of comments, focus on form, requests of clarifications, summarizing, etc. **less intrusive**. By using these amplification techniques, instructors and students can maintain seamless, productive communication.

2. Sound and visuals in written venues serve as **time savers**. Simultaneous commentaries in different media are thereby economical. They can also function as **L2 gatekeepers** as there is less need to revert to the native language when other target language means will do.

3. Sound and visuals in written venues are tools for instructors to render both form and meaning more **salient**.

4. Due to the proliferation of simple-to-use online tools, sound and visuals are easily **accessible**. They can be linked, embedded into the text or attached.

5. Digital natives are quite fluent in these forms of multimodal communication. Their **familiarity** with incorporating multiple messages in multiple modalities is part and parcel of their digital literacy and can, therefore, be put to good use in language education.

In written modes of communication, sound and visuals used in addition to voice can play different roles in the task:

- task toolkits;

- focusing on meaning;

- focusing on form;

- additional comments on the topic;

- modeling.

Links to videos, audios and images, embedded videos and sound files, emoticons, drawings and arrows are just some of the ways visuals and sound supplement and support written modes of instruction.

Non-intrusiveness

Images or sounds can be used to avoid intrusiveness. At the same time, they can serve highly effective instructional purposes, such as reminders of certain grammar, vocabulary or pronunciation issues that arise in the written mode. Sound and visuals can link students to previous knowledge and help to cement it into their developing repertoires. In the example below (Figure 112), a student conjugated the verb incorrectly and the instructor linked him to a chart she uses in class that she found online at http://www.musicalspanish.com/tutorial/newsletters/verbs-chart.gif.

S: Habla español.
T: Cuán de bien usted habla español (*link to the conjugation chart*)

Here are the basic patterns for conjugating regular present tense verbs:

infinitive ending →	AR	ER	IR
	hablar to speak	**ver** to see	**vivir** to live
	-o hablo	**-o** veo	**-o** vivo
	-as hablas	**-es** ves	**-es** vives
	-a habla	**-e** ve	**-e** vive
	-amos hablamos	**-emos** vemos	**-imos** vivimos
	-an hablan	**-en** ven	**-en** viven

Figure 112 Non-intrusive visuals in written modes

References to grammar songs or songs related to grammar can be an effective yet non-intrusive way to remind students of a rule without directly pointing to it. In the following example (Figure 113), an ESL instructor adds a link to a song that students had listened to in class.

S: I took a apple and a banana.
T: I also took an apple but I did not take a banana. (*link to the grammar song on English articles supplied with lyrics on http://gardenofpraise.com/mugram7.htm*)

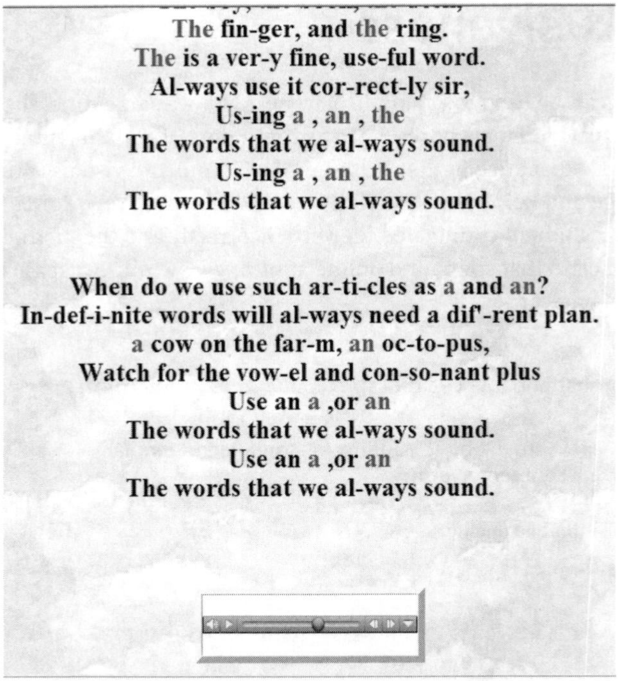

The fin-ger, and the ring.
The is a ver-y fine, use-ful word.
Al-ways use it cor-rect-ly sir,
Us-ing a , an , the
The words that we al-ways sound.
Us-ing a , an , the
The words that we al-ways sound.

When do we use such ar-ti-cles as a and an?
In-def-i-nite words will al-ways need a dif'-rent plan.
a cow on the far-m, an oc-to-pus,
Watch for the vow-el and con-so-nant plus
Use an a ,or an
The words that we al-ways sound.
Use an a ,or an
The words that we al-ways sound.

Figure 113 Non-intrusive sound in written modes

Time savers and L2 gatekeepers

As a means of saving time when learners are actively engaged in authentic target language conversation, pointing or linking to the oral or visual version of lexical items with which they are struggling can serve to save time and discourage learners from reverting to a common L1. In the following example, an elementary Russian II student uses the word 'nature' incorrectly by transliterating the English word 'натура' [nature; spirit; essence; character; personality], which does not fit the current context. The instructor implicitly corrects this mistake by using meaning/form-focused feedback. In her reply, she uses the word 'природа' [nature] and emphasizes the real meaning of this word by listing its components. To insure the transparency of the meaning for the student, the instructor adds a link to a youtube video about nature in Switzerland.

S: Сейчас, я живу в Атланте. Это большой город! Но, мне нравятся жить в деревне. Натура и очень красивая погода в деревне. Может быть, я могу жить в Европе! Я хочу маленький дом с прекрасная семья. [Now I live in Atlanta. It's a big city! But I like to live in a country. There are essence (*incorrect use of word*) and a very beautiful weather in a country. Maybe I can live in Europe! I want a little house and a great family.]

T: Да! Я тоже так думаю. Природа в деревне красивая. Жить в Европе в деревне очень хорошо, например, во Франции, недалеко от Парижа, или в Швейцарии. Там тоже красивая природа: лес, горы, цветы, озёра, реки, как в этом видео – Швейцария. Природа на Youtube. [Yes! I think so too. Nature (*correct word*) in the country is beautiful. To live in Europe in the country is very good, for example, in France not far from Paris or in Switzerland. There is also beautiful nature (*correct word*): forest, mountains, flowers, lakes, rivers... like in this video – Switzerland. Nature on YouTube (*link to the video on* http://www.youtube.com/watch?v=3S_zAzrvFOg *and a screenshot from the video*).] (Figure 114)

Figure 114 Written venues with sound and visuals

Acquiring new vocabulary in written environments using multiple modalities can be extremely time saving and effective. In addition to learning from text models of spontaneous real-life text-based communication, students can figure out the meaning of new words from images and familiarize themselves with their pronunciation and additional meanings from links.

T: Do you play soccer?
S1:   No not really... I played soccer when I was on high school.
S2:   Kenta you are probably a sumo restler ha ha
T: No, he is not a sumo wrestler (*link to a dictionary and pronunciation guide* http://dictionary.reference.com/browse/sumo; *an image of a sumo wrestler*). (Figure 115)

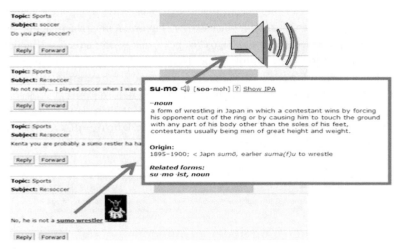

Figure 115 Sound and visuals save time

Salience

Inserting a link to a video clip of a grammar lesson can be another non-intrusive yet salient way to point to an error in the student's utterance. In the following text-based forum a group of ESL students discuss the topic 'If you were an animal, which animal would you be?' While the discussion keeps going on the main topic, the link to a video grammar lesson as a means of directing a student to a grammar rule, does not interrupt the discussion (Figure 116). It does, however, improve the chances of the implicit correction being attended to.

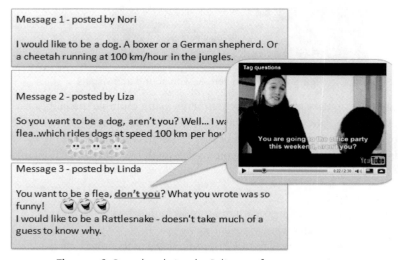

Figure 116 Sound and visuals. Salience of grammar points

S1: I would like to be a dog. A boxer or a German shepherd. Or a cheetah running at 100 km/hour in the jungles.

S2: So you want to be a dog, *aren't you?* Well... I want to be a flea..which rides dogs at speed 100 km per hour...in jungles. (*smiley faces*)

T: You want to be a flea, *don't you?* (*link to a youtube grammar video on tag questions with written and oral models*) What you wrote was so funny! (*laughing faces*) I would like to be a Rattlesnake – doesn't take much of a guess to know why.

Accessibility

While very effective environments for the development of linguistic fluency, written venues are viewed as lacking opportunities for learners to develop oral skills. With newer digital technologies, this issue is easily solved. **Task toolkits**, models, separate words in a text message, comments and notes can be partially or fully voiced and visualized for better student perception and comprehension. Sounds and visuals can be linked or embedded to make them accessible at any moment to be accessed as many times as students need. In the following chat activity 'How do you prepare for a birthday party?' a Japanese instructor in an elementary Japanese II class provides a **task toolkit** that includes both written and oral models of monologs discussing birthdays from a previous lesson (Figure 117). By clicking on the links English, Grammar, Key Vocabulary and Additional Vocabulary, students can quickly refer to the appropriate portions of the lesson and receive both textual and aural input to help them move along with the chat-based discussion.

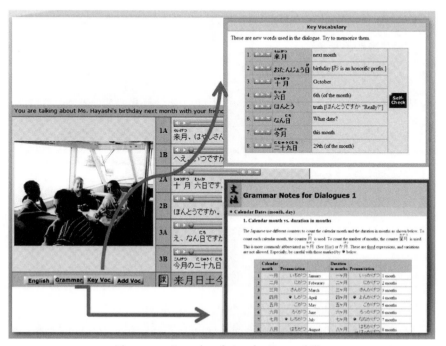

Figure 117 Sound and visuals. Accessibility

Familiarity

Digital natives quickly pick up on the advantages of internet technologies and implement visual components in their text-based chat activities on the spur of the moment. They are used to browsing websites, online dictionaries, image databases, etc. The current generation of L2 learners does not hesitate to incorporate multimodalities into their class work. In this example, students in an elementary Russian II class work in pairs to discuss their national heritage. The instructor provides them with a visual **task toolkit** for the oral activity that students have used in another lesson. Directions are supplied via the instructor's voice. She also uses visuals with arrows pointing to the words and images, hints for the correct answers, emoticons and question marks that she draws on the whiteboard (Figure 118). Students discuss their heritage and make reference to the google image database to explain and illustrate their posts.

S1: Кто твои бабушка и дедушка? [Who are your grandma and grandpa?]

S2: Моя бабушка русская. Мой дедушка украинец. [My grandma is Russian. My grandpa is Ukrainian.]

S1: Что украинец значит? [What does "Ukrainian" mean?]

S2: (link to the image with Ukrainian people) http://cache.virtualtourist.com/895408-Ukrainian_women_in_traditional_dress-Ukraine.jpg

S2: (link to the image with the map of Ukraine and nearby countries) http://www.unc.edu/~noblitt/fall2006/svetlanav_UKRAINE.gif

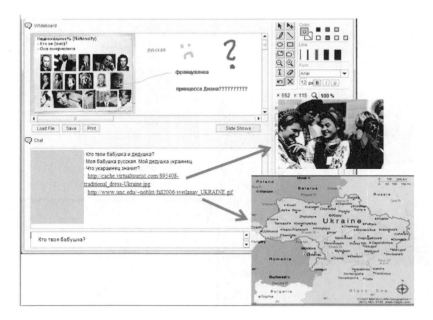

Figure 118 Written venues with sound and visuals

The use of emoticons, icons and avatars is also something to which contemporary students are accustomed while communicating in written modes. The example below shows how a discussion about global warming is spiced up with icons representing such abstract concepts as approval, disapproval, laughter, youth and noticing people (Figure 119). These icons help amplify meaning in a fun, playful manner.

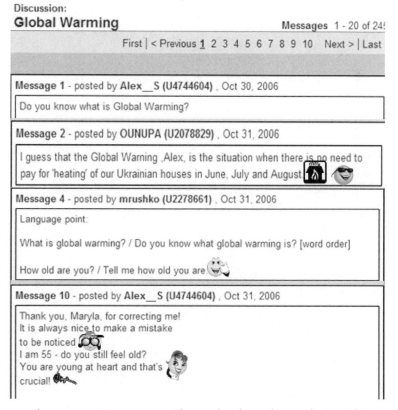

Figure 119 Written venues with sound and visuals. Familiarity with icons

In short, written environments for online language learning and teaching can be greatly augmented using multiple modalities when their use makes good, pedagogical sense. The preceding examples attempt to illustrate some of the methods of written instructional conversation that make use of sounds and visuals to just such ends.

8

Continuing the conversation

- Affordances for language teaching and learning in the four environments are summarized.

- Contextualizing the five skills in online language education is taken up.

- Various designs for language curricula are presented.

- The chapter discusses elements of good instructional design.

- The craft of language teaching is revisited and future directions suggested.

Continuing the conversation

Objectives/Preview

- Recap of the four environments and their affordances for:
    - The five skills;
    - Building online language learning curricula.
- Review instructional design essentials;
- Consider the craft of online language educators.

It should be clear from the range of illustrations and examples in the preceding chapters that our division of the telecommunications environments presented and illustrated into four discrete types is an arbitrary division. Oral, written, synchronous and asynchronous modes can, of course, be combined in any number of ways that make pedagogical sense. So, if a language course is conducted completely or partially online, instructors can make use of any of these modes and combinations of these modes to best effect the instructional outcomes they desire. In our examples and illustrations of online language learning in action, we hope to have captured this versatility of modalities while focusing on the central element of effective online language education: the instructional conversation.

We now discuss the affordances of online instructional venues in terms of the five language skills, one or more of which are the aim of any online language learning task: reading, listening, composition, speaking, pronunciation and intonation.

Reading

Reading any target language text can be greatly facilitated and the experience amplified thanks to internet resources. Not only can learners access highly contemporary and motivating authentic reading matter, but they can also engage others who read the text in conversation about it. Periodicals of all kinds have blog extensions whereby readers share thoughts and expand on the focal text. This opening up discussion of a text to the world is a powerful aspect of learning to read in a second language and in many ways encourages the integration of written and spoken language production as a matter of course. Plays, short stories, anime, manga, how to sites, even commercial shopping sites in the target language allow ready access to authentic text and a wide range of genres.

The oral online environments are excellent venues for reading instruction at the beginning levels. Learners can access texts in both written and oral modes. Simultaneously listening and reading serves to acclimate learners to the oral and written systems of the new language while digital tools can assist in replaying, annotating and providing glosses and translations. Target language reading practice at all levels can be encouraged through tasks and assignments that require information location, retrieval and synthesis; tasks and assignments shaped around focal target language texts; oral and written discussions about prose and fiction pieces learners have read on their own, etc.

Listening

It is an understatement that opportunities for independent listening are vast on the internet. Target language podcasts, some specifically tailored for learners of the language, some simply authentic listening material for pleasure and/or instruction, are readily available for free download onto students' computers and/or portable digital players. Assigning learners to listen to target language files with specific accompanying tasks to accomplish (write a summary, letter in response, present key points to the class, assemble a semantic net) is an effective independent learning activity. Moreover, as we discovered in our chapters on online learning environments that make use of teacher and learner voices, archives of classes whereby learners can review audio sequences of the instructional activities in which they engaged (or missed for some reason), archived audio can be a key learning tool. Songs and dramatic readings are excellent pleasure listening that learners can be encouraged to listen to in their free time to improve overall target language listening comprehension.

Practice with listening in the target language can be directly supported in all four instructional environments. Oral synchronous is clearly an aural intensive medium where learners must work to understand both the instructor and fellow students in real time. Nonetheless, as we have demonstrated throughout, there are numerous visual and textual supports to facilitate the kind of contextualized comprehension that language acquisition thrives on. Oral asynchronous modes are particularly useful in that digital voice files can be reviewed and annotated according to the task and to individual learner needs. The written modes can be used for listening work as well by linking or attaching files of plays, short dramatic readings, poetry readings, songs, brief film tracks, radio pieces and the like. Written tasks and discussions about these recordings motivate careful, purposeful listening and review.

Composition

Most contemporary learners or digital natives are aware of the plethora of resources available to them as they compose in the target language. Nonetheless, raising that awareness and guiding learners in locating and making intelligent use of online resources in their writing is another role of the online language educator. Instructional guidance is also critical as students develop their theses and make decisions about what aspects of their topic need definition and expansion. Instructors can also guide second language writers in pointing to linguistic resources needed in composing while guiding them to authentic models to gain a sense of thematic voice (e.g. refutation, concession, wry critique) in target language exposition. Development of writerly voice in the target language can be shaped with the help of instructors who assist with organizational and language choices throughout the composing process. This composition support and instruction can take place as private writing conferencing online or public. Developing a written piece in a public forum can assist not only the writer, who benefits from multiple perspectives and varied input, but also assists others in the class with their own writing efforts. Posting drafts, providing feedback and responding to successive developments is an enriched and enriching form of second language writing development.

Like the oral mode for listening, the written mode for composition is a logical pairing. However, using voice stimulus, aural feedback and oral synchronous discussion around a writing assignment or piece of student written work can be pleasing and stimulating. Hearing the voices of the instructor and peers talking about one's work can motivate a writer a great deal. The fluidity and spontaneity of readers' reactions can be more informative than shorter, more composed written feedback. Of course, both oral and written feedback are valuable to those writing in a new language.

Multimodal composition – whereby language learners combine written, visual and oral information into a public product – is something that digital natives are quite versed at doing in their native language, but can also do in the target language. Multimedia presentations that include critical writing practice in condensing messages and rendering them attention-getting and attractive, as well as readily comprehensible, can be very powerful composition assignments in any of the four environments.

Speaking

It has long been held that asynchronous and synchronous text exchanges more resemble the spoken form of language than the written, though some have argued that their character lies somewhere between the two. Nevertheless, when learning a language, comprehending and generating a textual version of a conversation is without question valuable. Learners can only benefit from *seeing* the language used in instructional conversations. In our two oral/ aural environments, oral synchronous and oral asynchronous, we saw how learners could engage in speaking activities independent of text if they so chose. These forms of speaking practice – with, without text, in real or delayed time – are powerful, perhaps more powerful, than in f2f environments due to the following: resources to assist comprehension and production, time to process, multiple and varied voices using the target language productively and, perhaps most importantly, 100% opportunity to participate unlike the live classroom where the floor is typically monopolized by a few more aggressive learners.

In oral synchronous and asynchronous environments, practice in speaking the target language can be easily orchestrated. In both written and oral environments, as we have seen, instructional conversations can serve to focus learner attention on correct production in terms of form, lexis and pronunciation while keeping the focus on authentic communication. We have also seen how speaking practice can be greatly facilitated by the presence of concise **task toolkits** to establish the focal language to be used.

Pronunciation and intonation

Even though the logical choice of venue for a focus on pronunciation and intonation would be the oral synchronous and oral asynchronous environments, the written environments can be used as well (see our examples throughout where visual highlighting is used to emphasize pronunciation and intonation). The beauty of all online environments in this regard is that learners struggle to a varying degree with new sounds in the target language. Rather than spending whole class time working with individual learners on their specific oral challenges, learners can be 'taken aside' and provided remediation in the way of recorded sound files to practice and visual resources that illustrate the physiological positioning of the mouth to reference. Indeed, pronunciation coaching sessions can be set up for single or small groups of learners to focus on specific phonological issues in speech production. For those struggling with the sounds of the new language, relaxed listening to recorded audio sequences should be recommended so learners can become familiar with the sound system and its contours in a casual manner.

In short, both asynchronous and synchronous and both written and oral venues can be used to great advantage to focus learner attention on the sounds and sound combinations in the target language while providing tailored practice in producing those sounds and patterns with which each individual learner needs support.

Designing online language learning curricula

When starting out to teach partially or fully online, following an existing, set curriculum provided by your institution or a textbook may be the most straightforward way to begin. By doing so, the burden of macro design is left to someone else thus freeing you to concentrate on smaller online task design, orchestration and assessment, the heart of instructional processes. Once this aspect is fluent and comfortable, you can take on the job of developing part or whole online curricula for your language courses.

Developing tailored curricula for individual or groups of language learners is a hefty undertaking with much room for creativity in selection and fashioning of content. The identities and learning purposes of a group of students will determine content and assist you in making curricular decisions along the way. Language learning curricula can be viewed as any one or combination of the following.

Current events-based

Assembling reading, writing, discussing and undertaking language learning activities around current events, events of the target culture and/or global culture, is a stimulating approach to curricular design. There is no shortage of readily available, up to the minute current news programming to which an online course or online component of a course can link and/or be constructed around. Indeed, many national and international broadcasting news agencies now have web support for learners of the language of broadcast that include linguistically simplified summaries, glossaries, comprehension exercises and content-based drills and games.

The multimedia aspect of news programming – the availability of high quality video, commentary and writing – make this model of curriculum design even more attractive. A particularly powerful feature of this approach is the authenticity of the language used as it is designed for a wide audience. Additionally, if your learners live in a geographical area where they have access to native speakers or, in the case of English learners, speakers of English as a lingua franca, current events are guaranteed to be a popular topic of everyday conversation.

Literature-based

Using the literature of the target language/culture has long been a mainstay of language education. Using literature as the organizing piece for language curricula, especially online, makes very good sense. Novels, short stories, poetry and critical essays can be discussed, annotated, resourced, referenced with any number of language tasks built around the literature itself. Numerous internet sites provide free and open access to literary works both complex and simple for lower proficiency learners. The possibilities for mining the depths of craft, content and cultural aspects of literature are well recognized. Online, these expand to include any and all cultural and linguistic references and expansions to amplify the reading and discussion experience.

Culture-based

In language education, we refer to Big C culture and Little c culture. Big C encompasses the great art, architecture and literature of the target culture. So, when learning Spanish, for example, the contents of El Prado or the stories of Don Quixote would be focal as far as Big C culture goes. Little c culture, on the other hand, is the culture of everyday life: buying bread at the market, finding a plumber, making a tortilla. Contemporary language curricula, while placing more emphasis on Little c culture, tend to include both.

When designing an online course, you can just as well have your learners visit a virtual mall or marketplace in the target culture as the largest art gallery or museum. In either case, the content is worked for its linguistic and motivational potential, keeping in mind again the learners and their particular goals in learning the language. If they never intend to visit the target culture, then both Little c and Big C can be incorporated for their interest, motivation and authentic value. On the other hand, if they plan to visit, study or work in the target culture, then the content can be tailored to those future needs.

Theme-based

Themes or topics are popular focal organizing devices for language curricula design. Textbooks most often use themes for modules or chapters that organize around a unified idea. Themes can be large life issues such as love, justice, freedom, etc. They can also be more narrow and practically oriented: vacations, food, job interviews, etc. The choice of theme depends a great deal on the age group and interests of students. For example, if students are school-age, using themes from the academic content areas is a useful technique. If students are studying the language for the purpose of emigrating to the target culture, themes of everyday life may be the best focus.

Of course in online environments, such themes can be complemented by existing multimodal materials and resources to enliven and expand them. The depth to which your class explores particular themes is only a matter of setting a course, defining requirements and providing language learning activities built in and around the themes selected.

Grammar-based

A long-standing tradition in language education has been to design curricula that use grammar – from easiest to most difficult – as the organizing structure. Most recently, popular curricula are built around a combination of themes and the grammatical structures that naturally occur within them. Using a set progression of grammatical structures as a guide when designing curricula – grammar-based or otherwise – is a useful approach and one that can satisfy learners' needs to see a measure of progress.

Specific purposes-based

More often students are studying a new language for use in specific contexts, for specific purposes. This could be anything from basic tourism purposes to relocating in the target culture and using the language to undertake one's profession: e.g. language for dentistry, language for information technology, language for international business. When it is the case that students need this kind of language for specific purposes, it is the responsibility of the instructor to design and implement a curriculum accordingly.

For many languages, specific purposes language curricula exist and can be located on the internet. For many other languages, these do not. The instructor then becomes a discourse detective and analyst, investigating the contexts in which the special purposes language will be used, analyzing its structures, vocabulary and functional aspects, and rendering these into productive online activities for learner mastery.

Functions-based

Functions are categories of the ways that meanings get realized in language. They are the basic units that represent how we do things with language to effect change. These communicative acts consist of greeting, leave-taking, promising and apologizing and are, as many have argued, extremely central to overall language proficiency. If we wish to agree with someone in English, for example, we say 'I agree with you', an act which performs a specific function.

In online venues, language functions can be taught explicitly by appearing and being referred to in the **task toolkit**. There are also language functions that naturally occur in online conversations that are representative of how language is used in live contexts. For example, when instructors direct learners' attention in online forums, the language function is identical to that of *inviting* or *suggesting*: 'Have a look at Part A of the **task toolkit**' 'You can find out more about the use of this word here <link>'. Likewise, because of the higher chance for misunderstanding in online venues, opportunities naturally arise for apologies and responding to apologies: 'I didn't see the link you provided, I'm so sorry I missed it'.

Contemporary language syllabi often include language functions as these intersect with themes, culture and even grammar, but rarely serve as a single organizing curricular tool. When undertaking curriculum design, oftentimes the logic of including foci on specific language functions becomes clear by virtue of the content studied.

Additionally, your curriculum can be linearly and cumulatively designed, organized in a spiraling or recycling fashion or as time-sensitive chunks (as with current events, for example). What is important when making use of online environments is to design using a few heuristics. In the case of blended formats, these include taking optimal advantage of the online and live venues for that which they work best. Time, access to resources and spoken, written and recorded texts are key considerations. Likewise, making optimal use of environmental affordances for fully online courses is a must. Apart from these venue-specific considerations, how the curriculum is sectioned, the amount of time you allot for each section and how much time you indicate that learners should spend on a given activity are considerations that of necessity vary according to the goals, requirements and learners involved.

Instructional design

The design of instruction to stimulate, guide and sustain powerful online instructional conversations is something we hope was well illustrated via the examples provided in Chapters 2–7. We have summarized the principles that guide these successful online language learning activities in the box below.

Key Instructional Design Principles

- clear objectives, visible during learning activity

- structure and sequence

- well designed tasks

- carefully calculated group strategies

- exploitation of teachable moments

- engaging instructional conversations

- consistent evaluation rubrics

- targeted inclusion of stimulating, authentic voices and materials

- continuous, active instructional presence

- granting learners active responsibilities

- atmosphere of learning community, mutual respect, love of learning

- cooperation and flexibility above competition

- continual awareness and monitoring of learner trajectories

These principles underlie the thinking, planning and implementation of online components and courses for effective language education. The overarching principle that pertains to curricular and instructional design is *flexible responsiveness*. Continually tuning in to learners, their developmental trajectories, and the teachable moments that arise through the instructional opportunities you design is by far the most important aspect of online language teaching. After all, predominant theories and practices in language education see learners' language development as a dynamic 'in flight' set of processes. These have variously been called acquisition processes, languaging (Swain, 2006; Tocalli-Beller & Swain, 2007), development through interaction, and the like. Contemporary language learning is thereby about productive, socially motivated language *use* as a route to mastery. As we have illustrated throughout this text, online instructional environments can be viewed as particularly well suited for orchestrating these processes in a number of respects. Each of the four environments that we explored has its own particular attributes and affordances that can support and amplify the kinds of powerful instructional conversations widely viewed as essential to language development. In addition, by virtue of being online, access to vast resources, including ways the target language is used in myriad contexts can be fluently referred to and made use of by both learners and their instructors. By observing how online language learning tasks are designed and guided by seasoned educators, we can conclude that the key to successful instruction rests, without a doubt, on the skills, creativity and craft of language teachers.

The craft of language education

Excellent language teaching is often likened to arranging and conducting a complex musical score. Add the dramatic element (the language learning task and its orchestration) and the enterprise begins to resemble opera! Layers and layers of complex, interlocking decisions must be made and actions taken while the overall objective/purpose of a language learning activity anchors those decisions.

Historically, we have had few tangible records of excellent language teaching practices, save a handful of devoted pupils who sat at their masters' feet and recorded their every word. With electronic communications and online teaching, however, we now have a powerful window on the world of seasoned, talented language educators at work, educators whom we can study and from whom we can learn about instructional conversations that work to further students' language development.

Playfulness

As you may have observed while reading examples of online language learning in this book, learning new languages can be a lot of fun and nowhere else in modern life is fun more likely than on the internet. Two aspects of contemporary online life are relevant in this regard: gaming and social networking. When we design and orchestrate online learning activities, indeed entire courses, these two elements can be integrated with very positive results. From the world of online gaming, for example, we have learned that what keeps players fully engaged is the fact of continuous feedback, a phenomenon that has been casually termed the Nintendo Effect. What could be a better approach to language education than to keep learners continually alert, interested and motivated to engage material for problem solving? From social networking we have learned that a major, if not *the* major attraction of the internet is *human* responsivity. In both the cases of gaming and social networking, there is often the element of language play or playing with language. One need only have a look at the ways that language is played with in online communications to see this in action. As language educators, we can incorporate the element of play and playfulness easily into our online instructional practices. In fact, a great deal of language play outside of language education involves the manipulation of forms and meanings as well as resolving incongruities, things that we do in language instruction as a matter of course!

In many instances, getting the joke requires sophisticated mastery of the language of the joke. However, jokes and funny stories can be equally appreciated at lower levels of proficiency with some help. It's worth the effort. Playfulness can indeed help in promoting a strong sense of group membership – an essential element of successful online practices (Darhower, 2002). By literally sharing the joke, students from disparate corners of the planet can experience a sense of belonging. Moreover, research has pointed to play as an important part of cognitive development, especially the development of cognitive flexibility, a required trait for successful language learning. This kind of flexibility is also supportive in group language learning activities, both online and off. Finally, it is viewed as a fruitful aspect of second language learning overall as regards student persistence in learning a new language well (Anthony & Meskill, in progress). After all, knowing a language well means being able to manipulate it, to play with it to the desired effect.

The future is now?

Opportunities for learning have greatly augmented with telecommunications developments. To no discipline is this more relevant than language education. With interaction with others being the central element of successful mastery of new languages, these online learning opportunities are doubly attractive. Add to the mix the fact that one can immerse oneself in target language cultures through simulated environments, and the future is indeed now for those wishing to learn a new language. However, as we hope to have illustrated throughout this text, the critical player in the language learning alchemy remains talented educators; educators who plan, orchestrate and guide language learning through productive instructional conversations. Regardless of the medium, the tools and the algorithms, language development depends on humanware; that is, you, the teacher.

Chapter discussion questions

1. In designing a curriculum, what is the best way to find out learners' needs and interests?

2. Having determined learners' needs and interests, how might you proceed to determine a macro design for the curriculum?

3. In developing a language curriculum, how do instructional conversations come into play?

End of chapter activity

Consider the following as metaphors for language teachers:

- Tour guide

- Conductor

- Doctor

- Systems analyst

- Director

- Shill

With a partner, discuss the salience of these metaphors and, based on what you have learned about teaching and learning online, add to the list with some of your own.

Further reading

DeKeyser, R. (2007) Skill acquisition theory. In B. Van Patten and J. Williams (eds) *Theories in second language acquisition: An introduction* (pp. 97–114). New York: Routledge.
Goertler, S. and Winke, P. (2008) *Opening doors through distance language education: Principles, perspectives, and practices.* San Marcos, TX: The Computer Assisted Language Instruction Consortium Monograph Series Volume 7.
Goodfellow, R. and Hewling, A. (2005) Re-conceptualizing culture in virtual learning environments: From an 'essentialist' to a 'negotiated' perspective. *E-Learning* 2 (4), 356–368.

Lamy, M. and Hampel, R. (2007) *Online communication in language learning and teaching.* New York: Palgrave MacMillan.

Lyster, R. (2007) *Teaching language through content.* Amsterdam: John Benjamins.

Markee, N. (1997) *Managing curricular innovation.* New York: Cambridge University Press.

Tomlinson, B. (2004) *Developing materials for language teaching.* New York: Continuum.

Ur, P. (1991) *A course in language teaching.* New York: Cambridge University Press.

Van Ek, J. (1990) *The threshold level in a European Unit-credit system for modern language learning by adults.* Strasbourg: Council of Europe.

Warner, C. (2004) It's just a game, right? Types of play in foreign language CMC. *Language Learning of Technology* 8 (2), 69–87.

References

Anthony, N. and Meskill, C. (in progress) Humor in online language education.

Darhower, M. (2002) Interactional features of synchronous computer-mediated communication in the intermediate L2 class: A sociocultural case study. *The Computer Assisted Language Instruction Consortium Journal* 19 (2), 249–277.

Swain, M. (2006) Languaging, agency and collaboration in advanced second language proficiency. In H. Byrnes (ed.) *Advanced language learning: The contribution of Halliday and Vygotsky* (pp. 95–108). London: Continuum.

Tocalli-Beller, A. and Swain, M. (2007) Riddles and puns in the ESL classroom: Adults talk to learn. In A. Mackey (ed.) *Conversational interaction in second language acquisition* (pp. 143–167). New York: Oxford University Press.

Free online teaching spaces

Dimdim
http://dimdim.com

Moodle
http://moodle.org

Nicenet
http://www.nicenet.org/

Learning Activity Management System (LAMS)
http://www.lamsinternational.com/

Bbwiki
http://bbwiki.com/

Pbworks
http://pbworks.com/

Glossary of terms

Asynchronous environments
Venues where messages are posted and read or listened to at any time, not synchronously.

Avatar
A 3-D graphic representing a participant in online environments.

Blended learning
A course designed to take place partially face-to-face and partially online.

Blog
An asynchronous space for posting public writings.

Calling attention to forms
Instructor (or a student) points out forms that a learner needs to be using.

Calling attention to lexis
Instructor (or a student) points out vocabulary words that a learners needs to be using.

Chat
Synchronous text-based communication.

CMC
Computer-mediated communication.

CMS
Course management system.

Corralling
Instructor (or a student) redirects learner's attention to specifics of language used.

Digital learning object
An online item specifically designed for instructional purposes.

Digital native
Learners born into the age of the internet.

Distance education
Teaching and learning via telecommunications.

Electronic portfolio
Cumulative, selected, annotated student work to demonstrate developing language competencies.

ELF
English as a lingua franca. English as it is used between non-native speakers of English.

f2f
Face-to-face learning as in the traditional brick and mortar classroom.

Focus on form
Instructional strategy whereby learners use language productively while focusing on specific language items that are pre-taught, monitored and become the focus of feedback.

Foreign/World language teaching and learning
Instruction that takes place outside of the target language culture.

Heritage language learner
A language learner who speaks the target language as his/her mother tongue but whose development in the language was usurped by the language of a new homeland at some point.

Hybrid course
Also, blended. A course partially taught online and partially face-to-face.

Hyperlink
A link to a file or url embedded within a text.

Instructional conversation
A conversational move that contributes to learners' language development.

L1
One's first language or mother tongue.

L2
The developing target language.

LMS
Learning management system. A suite of online tools used to develop an instructional environment.

LSP
Language for specific purposes.

Modeling
Instructor (or a student) models forms for learners to appropriate and use.

Online course
Typically used to describe a course that is 100% delivered via telecommunications.

Online teaching and learning
Teaching and learning using telecommunications.

NS
Native speaker, usually of the target language.

NNS
Non-native speaker, usually of the target language.

Podcast
Digital audio and video files available to play and download on the internet.

Providing explicit feedback
Instructor (or a student) explicitly points out mistakes and remediates.

Providing implicit feedback
Instructor (or a student) implicitly indicates a mistake.

Saturating
When a particular form (sets of vocabulary items and/or syntactic forms) is introduced and/or reinforced, the instructor saturates the conversation with these focal forms.

Second language teaching and learning
Language taught and learned within the target culture.

Second Life
One of many 3-D virtual worlds that can be used for synchronous teaching and learning.

Synchronous environments
Venues for teaching and learning in real time.

Tandem learning
A popular form of informal language learning whereby pairs or groups of learners teach and provide practice opportunities to one another in their respective languages.

Target language
The language under study.

Using linguistic traps
Instructor (or a student) traps a learner into using specific target language forms under study.

Index

Authors

Index

Subject